TRAVELS OF TERROR

KELLY FLORENCE

MEG HAFDAHL

STRANGE AND SPOOKY SPOTS ACROSS AMERICA

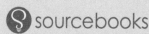

Published by Sourcebooks
P.O. Box 4410, Naperville, Illinois 60567-4410
(630) 961-3900
sourcebooks.com

Cataloging-in-Publication Data is on file with the Library of Congress.

Printed and bound in the United States of America.
VP 10 9 8 7 6 5 4 3 2 1

WE DEDICATE THIS BOOK TO
THE FEMALE PIONEERS OF TRAVEL
WHO BLAZED TRAILS AND
MADE HISTORY.

PORTLAND, OREGON

DULUTH, MINNESOTA

LOS ANGELES, CALIFORNIA

LAS VEGAS, NEVADA

AUSTIN, TEXAS

SALEM, MASSACHUSETTS

PROVIDENCE, RHODE ISLAND

ATHENS, OHIO

PITTSBURGH, PENNSYLVANIA

MARIETTA, GEORGIA

NEW YORK CITY, NEW YORK

ST. AUGUSTINE, FLORIDA

CONTENTS

INTRODUCTION

Some tourists seek pristine beaches and sparkling waters for the ultimate scuba dive. Others desire snowy peaks to ski down. And many more flock to the charming and innocent environs of theme parks. These are all lovely ways to spend a vacation, but we've always yearned for something more. Travel that speaks to our love of horror, history, and true crime. A distorted sort of Disney World for goths, where there is plentiful horror merch, macabre cocktails, and histories of badass women.

We've traveled the USA from coast to coast, searching the best haunted hotels, quirky museums, and immersive walking tours to spread the love of all things horror—from visiting the grave of the world's most devoted *Jaws* fan, to checking for ghosts outside the Amityville House. You'll get a taste of restaurants, bars, boutiques, and unique attractions that we're sure will make your horror heart happy. We hope this book inspires you to plan a spooky trip of your own.

OUR ORIGIN STORY

In 2001 (before GPS), we took our first horror-themed trip to Vancouver, British Columbia. Meg had moved away from the province six years earlier, so she was well aware of how robust the film industry had become in the area. Our reason for the expedition? To track down as many *The X-Files* (1993–2002) sites as we could find. We had met because of our love for the sci-fi–horror TV series, and it only seemed natural to spend our first trip as besties hunting down the locations. With just a map (yup, a paper one) and the book *X Marks the Spot: On Location with the X-Files* (1999) by Louisa Gradnitzer and Todd Pittson, we visited everything from a seedy bar seen in the episode "Never Again" to a cemetery where a peculiar body is exhumed in the pilot.

While other tourists were enjoying the orcas at the Vancouver Aquarium and the lush greenery of Stanley Park, we were hanging around industrial buildings for a peek at where our favorite fictional FBI agents once stood. And the best part? We had found each other, two friends who cared about the same spooky things. We were both willing to tromp through a forest to feel as if at any moment a creature would claw at our ankles (cue *The X-Files* theme).

Our adventures have continued over the years to destinations for fun—Paris, France, which included a creepy tour of the catacombs—and on work trips like Charlotte, North Carolina, for a *The Walking Dead* (2010–2022) convention to sell our books and wares. We've met the most interesting people who have given us tips and insight into the historical haunts and hidden gems they knew we would love.

In this book, you'll meet our social media friends Stephanie Sousa and her daughter Kira Feliciano, who we met up with in Fall River,

Massachusetts, a side trip on our quest to Salem. Being able to talk to locals of Fall River expanded on what we hoped to discover about the gothic finds in America. It puts into perspective that every city, burg, island, and corner of this country is home to darkness.

Both Kira and Stephanie recount growing up down the road from the Lizzie Borden House. As someone fixated on the Borden murders since she was young, Meg was struck by how casual they are about their hometown ghoulish legend. Sure, Kira has gone there for a school trip, but she's never spent a night in the bed-and-breakfast. Really, Fall River is more than Lizzie Borden to them, a lot more. It is where they went to school, got married, had children. Just as Kelly lives near Glensheen Mansion, where famous murders occurred (read about it in our Duluth, Minnesota, chapter), we all find ourselves in proximity to death. Which, sure, sounds really depressing, but it's actually kind of cool when you think of all the fascinating history that comes before us. Sometimes this local history, as in Stephanie and Kira's case, does involve ax murder.

Since our first gothic trip to Vancouver, we have devoted our careers to the complex genre that is horror, whether it be deconstructing female film tropes in our book *The Science of Women in Horror* (2020) or discovering what makes killers tick both in real life and on-screen in *The Science of Serial Killers* (2021). We're frightfully delighted to bring you our first travel book, sharing yet another creepy passion with those of you who walk on the dark side with us.

Read on and join us on our tour of America's best horror spots!

WELCOME TO

SALEM

MASSACHUSETTS

POPULATION: 44,819

SPOOKIEST THING TO HAPPEN HERE

Okay, yeah, this one is pretty obvious. The horror inclined come from far and wide to the witch capital of the world. We crave proximity to the dark history of Salem as well as the intoxicating hope that witches with magical powers *do* exist. When we first stepped foot onto Salem's cobblestones at the height of the Halloween season, the town provided exactly what we wanted: a haven for people like us. There were jack-o'-lanterns on nearly every step, sightseers dressed in costume, shop windows filled with posed skeletons wearing witchy hats. Basically, it's the happiest place on earth for us not-so-Disney inclined.

For stories of vengeful witches haunting the patriarchy, there are dozens of ghost tours operating in Salem. We think the creepiest thing to happen in Salem, though, is the witch trials themselves, namely the execution of nineteen accused witches in 1692. Not only were those killed greatly affected, but families were torn apart as hundreds were accused of worshipping the devil himself. A multitude of books, movies, and plays have been inspired by this tragedy, a hint of Europe's bloody witch slayings landing on American shores.

Nearly four hundred years later, humans are still fascinated, as evidenced by the large curious crowds in Salem. With aspects of cult-think, religious fervor, belief in the occult, and sanctioned murder, the Salem Witch Trials has it all. To learn more, go to the Salem Witch Museum or read *Six Women in Salem: The Untold Stories of the Accused and the Accusers in the Salem Witch Trials* (2013), in which Massachusetts author Marilynne K. Roach works to highlight the unique human stories of the Salem Witch Trials, not the stereotype or caricature of a Puritan woman. Also, Shirley Jackson, queen of all that is feminist and gothic, wrote a well-researched book for students, *The Witchcraft of Salem Village* (1956), a great start to understanding what happened.

HIDDEN GEM WE DISCOVERED

International Monster Museum

186 ESSEX STREET

Thanks to our friend (and super talented local fabric designer) Dan Pecci, we knew the International Monster Museum was worth a visit. It's hidden in a nondescript strip mall filled with T-shirt shops that, honestly, we wouldn't have given a second look. There was a lot of competition for our time in Salem, so having Dan's suggestion was priceless. If you've read any of our previous books like *The Science of Monsters* (2019), you'll know that we LOVE all kinds of monsters, especially when they come with folklore, history, and, yep, science. So, this museum is basically our dream: part haunted house, part anthropological museum of different cultures' baddies. Accompanying every depiction of a creature, such as Mary Shelley's famed monster from *Frankenstein* (1818), is information about its presence in culture. If you're not too scared to stop and read, that is. We may be hardened goth girls, but we screamed a couple of times. Our only complaint is that we wanted *way* more monsters.

 The iconic horror movie from director Steven Spielberg, *Jaws* (1975), was set in the fictional Amity, New York, but was filmed in Martha's Vineyard, located in Massachusetts.

MOST FAMOUS TRUE CRIME

The Salem Witch Trials, which led to the execution of innocent people, are undoubtedly the most famous case in Salem. But did you know there was a Salem murder about a century and a half later that inspired Edgar Allan Poe's 1843 masterpiece "The Tell-Tale Heart"?

A wealthy, retired ship captain, Joseph White, was found dead in his bed in his mansion on Essex Street. His skull had been crushed and his chest had been stabbed thirteen times in a particularly gruesome display with no discernible motive. A distant relative was convicted of the murder of the eighty-two-year-old after many twists and turns in the case. Even famed author Nathaniel Hawthorne wrote about the White mystery in his letters. You can visit the scene of the crime, now known as the Gardner-Pingree House, an official historic site. The house's website doesn't mention the murder, choosing to focus, instead, on the stunning architecture.

SPOOKY MOVIES AND BOOKS SET HERE

BOOKS

The House of the Seven Gables (1851) by Nathaniel Hawthorne

I, Tituba, Black Witch of Salem (1986) by Maryse Condé

A Head Full of Ghosts (2015) by Paul Tremblay

MOVIES

The Haunting (1963)

Hocus Pocus (1993)

The Witch (2015)

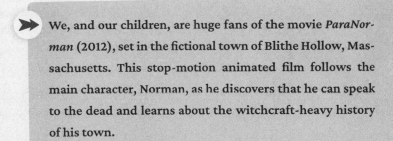

➤ We, and our children, are huge fans of the movie *ParaNorman* (2012), set in the fictional town of Blithe Hollow, Massachusetts. This stop-motion animated film follows the main character, Norman, as he discovers that he can speak to the dead and learns about the witchcraft-heavy history of his town.

 # WHAT TO DO

Salem Witch Museum

19½ NORTH WASHINGTON SQUARE

A highlight of our visit to Salem was the experience of touring the Salem Witch Museum. Originally a church, the museum was renovated in 1972 to educate the public about the history of the town, the witch trials, and the context surrounding them. Their mission: "to be the voice to the innocent victims of witch hunts, from 1692 to the present day. By understanding this history, through audiovisual displays, guided tours, educational events, and discussion, we strive to highlight the stories of the innocent individuals targeted during witchcraft trials." Be prepared to wait in line outside before your scheduled tour, then sit in darkness before witnessing a compelling reenactment of the witch trials in the former church. Through lighting, tableaux, and sound effects, we sat in a sold-out audience experiencing the display together. After the show, we toured other exhibits before leaving and were forever changed by the important information that was shared. We may have also mistakenly given our middle fingers to the statue across the street. Although Roger Conant might seem like he would have been one of the accusers during the trials, he was one of the founders of Salem (from the Hebrew word *shalom*, which means peace) and died before the witch trials took place, so our vengeance on his statue was probably misplaced.

Omen Psychic Parlor

184 ESSEX STREET

In 2022, we held a signing for
our book *The Science of Witchcraft*
at the Omen Psychic Parlor in
Salem. As the name suggests,
you can book a reading with a
psychic at the shop or peruse the store's
shelves, filled with everything from tarot
decks to candles. We met a number of people
who were shopping, passing by, and waiting to get their books signed
in the charming and conveniently located parlor. The back entrance to
this store leads into the mall where the International Monster Museum
is located as well as many other fun shops.

Charter Street Cemetery and the Pickman House

43 CHARTER STREET

Throughout our travels we've visited many cemeteries. They are usually
quiet places, an environment in which to reflect and contemplate. The
Charter Street Cemetery is quite the glaring opposite. As we were in Salem
in October, it was jam-packed with witchy people like us, eager to soak
up the gloomy vibes that only the town's oldest cemetery can provide.
Established before 1637, it is one of the oldest European graveyards in
the country, which is easily believed when you take in the crumbling
stones around you. "The first recorded reference to the Old Burying Point
(as Charter Street Cemetery was often known) was in 1637, when town
records show a local man named John Horne was given permission to

erect a windmill in the 'burial place.'" The next record appears in 1639, pertaining to the same windmill, and the same burial place, as the town: "ordered yt John Horne shall desist from his inclosure in ye bury all place: and yt ye town shall pay for a quarter of an acre when he hath bought ye same. except the Towne when they shall haue changed the buryall place shall alow him a portion of the same.'" Wow, John Horne sure was all about his cemetery windmill. Thanks to some really cool people with a lot of patience, there is an online database of all the gravestones at Charter Street, along with a photo of the site and information on the family of the deceased. This is handy, especially because the aged stones are hard to decipher. Some notable people interred there include Richard More, a passenger on the *Mayflower*; Barthlomew Gedney, who presided in court over one of the Salem Witch Trials; and Doraty Cromwell, a midwife who has the distinction of having the oldest known surviving gravestone at Charter Street. She died at age sixty-seven in 1673. Go, Doraty! Her stone is in remarkably good shape for its age.

Beside the small cemetery is the Pickman Building, built in the seventeenth century, now used as the visitor center for the graveyard. The Pickman family would be considered what we think of as "middle class," so their home is a good example of how many lived in the era. Interestingly, Lydia Pickman, wife of Samuel, the mariner who built the home, was asked to examine supposed "witch's marks" on some women accused during the witch trials. There's no indication as to why she was one of those asked, only that it meant she and her family were in good standing in the Salem community. "Witch-hunters often had their suspects stripped and publicly examined for signs of an unsightly blemish that witches were said to receive upon making their pact with Satan. This 'Devil's Mark' could supposedly change shape and color and was believed to be numb and insensitive to pain."

Inside the visitor center, you'll find information on those buried at Charter Street, general Salem history, colonial funerary exhibits, as well as a delightful gift shop that leans into what we love most about Salem: history, witches, and old-timey death.

 A statue of Elizabeth Montgomery from *Bewitched* can be found in Lappin Park in Salem next to a Little Free Library. The statue was unveiled in 2005 and features the actress as the character Samantha Stephens, sitting on a broom.

A Day Trip to the Emily Dickinson Museum

280 MAIN STREET, AMHERST

A two-hour drive from Salem is a pilgrimage that we believe is well worth the trip. Meg first became acquainted with the poet Emily Dickinson as a child because of her dad's deep fondness for Dickinson's work. He'd read Meg her poems and did his best to explain them. As she's gotten older, Meg's become a die-hard Dickinson fan. She explored the beauty of nature with the same emotional heft as her many musings on death. Dickinson's visceral poetry, borne from a quiet life in Massachusetts, prevails today, inspiring the recent Apple+ series *Dickinson* (2019–2021). And of course, her austere visage appears on countless items of goth merch, from coasters to earrings.

It wasn't until after her death that Emily Dickinson became an American icon of poetry, thanks to her sister's unearthing Emily's lifetime of work. Amherst, Massachusetts, is proud of its hometown goth girl, honoring her with a museum in her former home.

Before you plan your trip to Amherst, make certain that the museum is open. Due to the harsh New England winters, it is closed over the holiday season, not opening typically until mid-March. They also can't guarantee walk-ins, so buy your tickets on their website to ensure you get to tour Dickinson's house.

Our favorite activity offered at the museum is the "studio session," in which you can spend up to two hours sitting at the poet's desk in her bedroom, overlooking the same landscape that inspired some of the world's most revered poetry. It's pricey, but we figure if Dickinson's writing desk doesn't inspire your creativity, you may not be cut out for the arts. Just kidding, friend.

Once you've toured Emily Dickinson's home, it's a lovely ten-minute walk to West Cemetery to Dickinson's final resting place. If you want to show up in true Dickinson style, may we suggest a horse carriage adorned with black lace, out of which you can step and recite:

> *Because I could not stop for Death—*
> *He kindly stopped for me—*
> *The Carriage held but just Ourselves—*
> *And Immortality.*

A Day Trip to the Taunton State Hospital

HODGES AVENUE, TAUNTON

We wouldn't necessarily encourage you to go to an abandoned insane asylum. You'd really be asking for a ghost to follow you home. Or at least you'd get a case of tetanus. So, we're just going to let you know that the abandoned Taunton State Hospital, which is on the historic register, is about an hour and a half away from Salem, and it has a fascinating history steeped in one of the most famous female serial killers.

Built in 1854, the asylum was founded in an era when understanding of mental illness was fledgling at best. We go into greater detail on women's plight in institutions in our discussion of the Ridges (see the Athens, Ohio, chapter), but needless to say, Taunton State Hospital wasn't a place where women got better. Today, the crumbling leftovers of the hospital are closed to the public, but you can marvel at the edifice of what was once home to Jane Toppan.

Throughout our careers we've done quite a lot of research on serial killers, even comparing male and female in traits and modus operandi. One that stands out for us is Jane Toppan. Intrigued to know more, Meg read *America's First Female Serial Killer: Jane Toppan and the Making of a Monster* (2020) by Mary Kay McBrayer—in one sitting. McBrayer's research, as well as her empathetic yet realistic voice, is powerful.

In brief, Jane Toppan was an Irish immigrant who grew up impoverished and abused in Massachusetts. She went on to become a caretaker and nurse, killing at least twelve people under her "care." Several of these were close friends and even considered family. Toppan is a rare breed, as she confessed to authorities that there was a sexual thrill to her killings, which is not often an element in female serial killers. Just a few years after the Borden murders in Fall River, people were still reluctant to believe women were capable of cold-blooded murder. So, Toppan was deemed insane and committed to Taunton State Hospital, where she languished for over thirty years. She died within its walls, age eighty-four, in 1938.

If you decide you want to drive by and check out Taunton State Hospital, don't get it confused with the modern hospital of the same name. And if you break the rules and go inside, don't say we didn't warn you. From fire and disrepair, the buildings are dangerous. Also, if you don't heed our warning, we can't promise Jane doesn't haunt her former abode.

Hocus Pocus Filming Sites

98 WEST AVENUE (PIONEER VILLAGE)
161 ESSEX STREET (PEABODY ESSEX MUSEUM)

If you're a fan of the 1993 movie *Hocus Pocus*, you need to visit the multiple sites where the movie was filmed in Salem. The opening scenes of the film, featuring Binx (Sean Murray) as a human prior to being cursed as a cat, were filmed in the living-history museum of Pioneer Village, built in 1930. Tours are offered seasonally in the summer months. Another location, the Ropes Mansion, is owned by the Peabody Essex Museum. The gardens located in the rear of the mansion are free to visit and open to the public, and you'll recognize where Max (Omri Katz) attended a Halloween party in the film. Find locations on your own, or book a tour through one of the companies available—just make sure not to run amok!

WHERE TO SHOP

Copper Dog Books, Bookstore

272 CABOT STREET, BEVERLY

If you visit Beverly, Massachusetts, just over the bridge from Salem, make a stop at Atomic Cafe, which has a subtle nuclear aesthetic, grab a coffee to go, and then head next door to Copper Dog Books. Meg went a little crazy in Copper Dog, filling her too-full suitcase with a signed copy of Clay McLeod Chapman's supernatural thriller *The Remaking* (2019), about a horror film sparking real murder and mayhem in a northeastern town, and an epic T-shirt with a skeleton hand that says "Just One More Chapter..." among other goodies. Copper Dog holds events in-store, including signings and talks with heavy-hitting suspense novelists like Peter Swanson.

Paper Asylum, Comic Shop

260 CABOT STREET, BEVERLY

If you still have room for treasures, then head to the other side of Atomic Cafe in Beverly to Paper Asylum. We were impressed with their zany sticker collection, and as a graphic novel hound, Meg was happy to find the next installment of the dark fantasy Locke & Key series (2009) by Joe Hill, an author who lends his talent for emotionally charged horror to comics, while Kelly bought way too many unique collectibles for her kids (according to them, it was just enough).

Modern Millie, Boutique

3 CENTRAL STREET

In Salem, we had a great time shopping at the adorable boutique called Modern Millie. Initially drawn in by the Halloween-themed window displays, we immediately realized this shop was one of our favorites. Opened in 2006, Modern Millie started as a place to purchase vintage and modern consignment, and has now evolved to add vintage reproductions and accessories. The customer service was amazing as we browsed, wide-eyed at all the goth, spooky-themed, and beautiful pieces. Kelly miraculously left with only one item: a purse based on Sir Arthur Conan Doyle's Sherlock Holmes stories, which were published from 1887 to 1927. Complete with a 221B Baker Street re-creation with a hidden "door" opening, the purse will forever be a staple in her rotation of handbags. Although we could have left with the entire shop, we paced ourselves as best we could.

Nocturne, Boutique

18 FRONT STREET

With advice from a local friend, we made sure to stop by Nocturne. Established in 2022, the shop is "inspired by their lifelong love of Salem, alt-fashion, home decor, and the arts...an eclectic and whimsical boutique celebrating Salem's rich history and our magical world of artists and tradespeople." With delicious scents, witchy apparel, home goods, and accessories, we were in goth heaven (or hell?).

HausWitch, Boutique

144 WASHINGTON STREET

Our next stop in Salem was a shop featuring handmade products from independent makers from around New England. HausWitch includes elements of meditation, herbalism, and interior decorating to bring magic and healing into everyday spaces. The store is very welcoming and inclusive, and we were impressed with the variety of crystals, potions, and events the space holds. Check their website for what's happening next.

Emporium 32, Vintage Shop

6 CENTRAL STREET

We knew Emporium 32, with a line out the door, was a must-see while we were visiting Salem. Featuring a collection of everything from hats and other vintage wares to handmade items from over 125 local businesses and artists, the Emporium has an impressive abundance of gothic items to offer shoppers. We enjoyed wandering through the shop amid antiques and steampunk-inspired pieces.

WHERE TO STAY

Beverly

A more peaceful alternative to bustling Salem, Beverly, as we mentioned, is right across the bridge. We stayed in an Airbnb overlooking the picturesque bay, and it was an affordable way to be close to all the action. Like Salem, Beverly is highly walkable, with a plethora of history. With nearly every step, we encountered a house a house marked with a historical marker, a gothic church with razor-sharp spires, or a charming brick building restored to hold a boutique. One standout is the pale-yellow columned First Parish Church, founded in 1667. According to a faded plaque, the tower of the church was used as a cannon target for the British in 1775.

Hawthorne Hotel

18 WASHINGTON SQUARE WEST

Located conveniently in downtown Salem, the Hawthorne Hotel is the perfect place to book a stay while in Massachusetts. Established in 1925, the Hawthorne has seen over one million guests come through its doors, and its location is just steps from numerous restaurants, shops, and the Salem Witch Museum. The property is considered one of the most haunted hotels in America, with guests reporting unexplained noises, like barking dogs on floors where they shouldn't be allowed, the sighting of a ghostly woman, and objects—such as furniture—moving on their own. According to lore, the two most haunted rooms are 325 and 612. We enjoyed exploring the building, having drinks in the lobby, and being able to walk from the front doors to most of our destinations in Salem.

 The television show *Bewitched* (1964–1972) filmed a storyline with several episodes revolving around the town of Salem, featuring the episode arc of "The Salem Saga" which was filmed in 1970.

WHERE TO EAT

Toscana Bar Italiano

90 RANTOUL STREET, BEVERLY

In Beverly, stop by Toscana Bar Italiano for a delicious dinner, horror-themed drinks, and great service. We visited this restaurant more than once on our travels and were pleased with the quality of the food and the fun, welcoming atmosphere. We enjoyed fresh bread dipped in garlic-infused olive oil while we were waited on by a bartender resembling John Travolta. Turns out, he's a sci-fi author! Our main courses were also perfect, as we should have expected from an award-winning restaurant.

Hawthorne Hotel

18 WASHINGTON SQUARE WEST

While in Salem, whether you're staying at the Hawthorne Hotel or not, swing into the Tavern or Nathaniel's for a meal or drinks. Serving breakfast, lunch, and dinner, Nathaniel's is the perfect spot to take in a 1920s vibe and enjoy delicious food. The Tavern, a family-friendly restaurant with views of the Common, a public park, offers meals all day as well as drinks until 11 p.m. We enjoyed more than one meal here during our visit and would recommend it to all like us (i.e., lovers of the dark and spooky). A highlight? Seeing a table of people next to us, all fully garbed in horror-themed costumes.

A WOMAN YOU SHOULD KNOW

Tituba
(1674–UNKNOWN)

Many of us were introduced to Tituba in the 1996 film *The Crucible* (based on the 1953 Arthur Miller play) through her portrayal by actress Charlayne Woodard. She is the "other" in the puritanical white sphere of Salem, both in real life and in the film.

Brought to Salem by the town minister, Samuel Parris, from Barbados, Tituba, a slave in Parris's home, was one of the victims charged with a crime because of lies spread about her connection with witchcraft. As a woman of color and a slave, she was an immediate target because of her looks, language, and culture.

Tituba's past is cloaked in mystery, as it's not known if she was originally from Barbados, where Minister Parris found her. Some historians believe she was a native South American from the Arawak-Guiana tribe before she was sold into slavery to a plantation in Barbados.

However she came to be on the island, it is where she picked up her knowledge of local witchcraft, or Obeah, a West Indian belief system that involves spellcasting and healing.

For the strictly religious hamlet of Salem, Tituba's knowledge of Obeah would certainly have been unusual, and it was ultimately misunderstood during the trials as a sign of her being in cahoots with the devil.

One of Tituba's responsibilities was caring for the Parris children, two of whom started barking, blabbering, and crying hysterically after they played a fortune-telling game.

"Though she apparently had nothing to do with the girls' attempts at fortune telling (a grave sin in the Puritan religion), Tituba tried to help them. She baked a 'witchcake' from rye meal and urine and fed it to the girls. Parris, who had already begun praying and fasting in an attempt to cure the girls of what he saw as possession, became incensed when he heard Tituba had fed them the cake. He beat her in an attempt to get her to confess that witchcraft was the reason behind the girls' increasingly odd behavior." This witchcake (yep, they all have pee in them) was a common recipe used for healing that Tituba would've learned in Barbados. In her attempt to help, she unfortunately exposed her cultural background, which to Puritans was more than distasteful.

Alone in a foreign country and with no other choice, Tituba confessed to the crime of witchcraft. Later, it was revealed that she had told others that Samuel Parris had forced her to confess and to make up stories about others' involvement with the dark arts, on threat of death. After thirteen months in jail, Tituba was sold to an unknown slave owner. Considering nineteen people were executed, it's quite surprising that Tituba got away with her life. Historians have lost her trail after Salem, though it's likely she spent the rest of her life in slavery.

Unfortunately, in popular media, Tituba has often been seen as the catalyst that started the tragedy in Salem. This couldn't be further from the truth. She has been portrayed in art and literature as a devilish force who caught innocent girls in her web. Now that we are more informed about the interplay of racism, classism, xenophobia, and sexism, we can appreciate how unfairly Tituba was treated in 1692 and, later, depicted in drawings as evil and even as an instigator in *The Crucible*.

If you want to learn more about Tituba and Barbados's Obeah culture, we recommend the novel *I, Tituba: Black Witch of Salem*. It blends fiction and history to discuss the Salem Witch Trials from Tituba's point of view.

TRAVEL TIPS

1. Don't be afraid to pack your most gothic or Halloween-centric garb for Salem, no matter what time of year you are visiting. This is the place to let your freak flag fly and meet fellow horror enthusiasts.

2. If you're interested in a day trip away from Salem, check public bus routes. Sometimes they take more time than a car, but they can be more affordable and give you time for reading, napping, or streaming horror films on your phone.

3. Make sure to book your hotel or other overnight arrangements well in advance, especially if you plan to travel in the month of October. Hotels in Salem are filled many months ahead of time, so be flexible and don't be disappointed if you need to stay in a nearby town.

4. In the same vein, book any tickets for tours or experiences in advance for places like the Salem Witch Museum. Tickets sell out quickly, and only a handful are available the day of. You are able to book online (some tickets are on sale the night before at midnight), so be prepared to set an alarm and nab the tour time you'd like.

5. Airbnbs or vacation homes are a convenient way to book stays when you are traveling to the bustling town of Salem in the fall. Make sure to plan for transportation, like renting a car or using rideshares from adjacent towns, to make it on time to tours and attractions in Salem proper. We had no trouble finding quick rides to the places we wanted to visit while in Massachusetts.

LOS ANGELES

CALIFORNIA

POPULATION: 3.8 MILLION

SPOOKIEST THING TO HAPPEN HERE

While numerous horror movies have been filmed in California, legends abound of creatures that are purported to actually exist there. The Monster of Elizabeth Lake is said to have been created by the devil himself over the San Andreas Fault line. The creature is described as being over fifty feet long, sporting the wings of a bat, and having a nauseating stench. This pterodactyl or dragon like creature has been spotted by people over the years and is reportedly bulletproof.

HIDDEN GEM WE DISCOVERED

The Mystic Museum

3204 WEST MAGNOLIA BOULEVARD

The Mystic Museum in Burbank is the perfect place for any horror fan to spend an afternoon. With a recommendation from a friend, we ventured out after morning coffee to the museum and their other locations, the Victorian Seance Parlor and the Lost Toy Exhibit. Established in 2013, the museum hopes to keep horror alive through rotating themed art shows, interactive exhibits, and events. Seeing the vintage "lost toys" in person brought back a flood of memories to us both, with rooms set up like childhood bedrooms complete with Cabbage Patch dolls, *Ghostbusters* (1984) posters, and other memorabilia we collected as kids. The Seance Parlor had a plethora of items that could be absolutely haunted and were fun to explore, while a Ouija board moved on its own in the corner. There were numerous *The Evil Dead* (1981)–themed items for sale at the gift shop at the Mystic Museum, and we know you'll have a ball looking at all the horror exhibits, including a phone call with Ghostface himself. If you paid a little extra, the experience would even include a collectible plastic knife to stab into items within the museum to make the tableaux come to life. We lived out our slasher dreams witnessing scenes from *Friday the 13th* (1980), *Silence of the Lambs* (1991), *Candyman* (1992), *The Ring* (2002), and more during our visit. Stop by, explore, shop, and enjoy. You won't regret it.

MOST FAMOUS TRUE CRIME

From the famous unsolved murder case of Elizabeth Short, also known as the "Black Dahlia," in 1947 to the Richard Ramirez "Night Stalker" serial killings in the 1980s, California has a long history of true crime. One crime that people may not be aware of is the murders by Cordelia Botkin in 1898. She killed two women who lived across the country, without ever stepping foot in their residence. How? By using the U.S. Postal Service.

Botkin was sleeping with the husband of Mrs. Dunning, who later moved to Delaware, and was heartbroken when the man proclaimed he would never return to her. Botkin sent arsenic-laced candies to Mrs. Dunning through the mail, and six people partook in the indulgence, which they thought was from a family friend. They all became sick, and two people, Mrs. Dunning and Mrs. Deane, died. Evidence and handwriting analysis traced the package back to Botkin, who was sentenced to life in prison. Rumors spread that she became friendly with several guards and was able to leave the prison from time to time, but she eventually succumbed to "softening of the brain, due to melancholy" in 1910 at the age of fifty-six.

SPOOKY MOVIES AND BOOKS SET HERE

BOOKS

Carrie (1974) by Stephen King

Fledgling (2005) by Octavia E. Butler

Sundial (2022) by Catriona Ward

MOVIES

The Lost Boys (1987)

Scream (1996)

Us (2019)

Nope (2022)

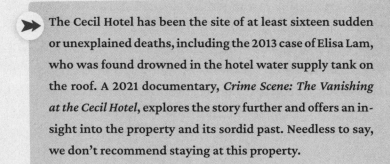

➤ The Cecil Hotel has been the site of at least sixteen sudden or unexplained deaths, including the 2013 case of Elisa Lam, who was found drowned in the hotel water supply tank on the roof. A 2021 documentary, *Crime Scene: The Vanishing at the Cecil Hotel*, explores the story further and offers an insight into the property and its sordid past. Needless to say, we don't recommend staying at this property.

Halloween Horror Nights at Universal Studios Hollywood

100 UNIVERSAL CITY PLAZA, UNIVERSAL CITY

With a new theme annually, the Universal Studios Halloween Horror Nights is a must-attend for every horror fan. Not your typical haunted house or theme park attraction, Halloween Horror Nights features highly curated and big budget experiences that honor and celebrate the films and television shows their displays are themed after. Past themes include *The Haunting of Hill House* (2018) and *The Texas Chainsaw Massacre* (1974) in 2021, The Horrors of Blumhouse in 2022, and the *Chucky* (2021–) Syfy television series in 2023. Although the lines might have been long, we enjoyed meeting fellow horror fans while waiting, shopping for horror-themed merch, and seeing hundreds of other people in Halloween costumes. If not visiting during the Halloween season, you'll still be able to see the Bates Motel from *Psycho* (1960) and other Universal monster exhibits.

The Hollywood Forever Cemetery

6000 SANTA MONICA BOULEVARD

The Hollywood Forever Cemetery was established in 1899. It's a stunning display of memorials honoring the dead, both famous and non-famous. Fans can leave trinkets and flowers at the graves of celebrities like silent film star Rudolph Valentino, who starred in *The Four Horsemen of the Apocalypse* (1921) and *The Sheik* (1921), and actor Anton Yelchin, star of *Star Trek* (2009) and *Fright Night* (2011). Others have stunning displays and memorials, including Judy Garland and Maila Nurmi (most commonly known as Vampira). Stop by the gift shop to pick up flowers to honor a loved one or favorite celebrity, and buy a copy of the guidebook, which will lead you through the vast cemetery, where majestic peacocks dwell, and where impressive monuments, inside and out, memorialize those who have gone before us. We couldn't help but get emotional as we saw all the lovely tributes by families, friends, and in some cases fans for the deceased.

Some notable ceremonies and events take place in the cemetery, including a celebration of the life of Rudolph Valentino. On August 23, the anniversary of Valentino's death, the famed "Lady in Black," veiled and dressed in all black, leaves a single red rose at his grave. This reportedly started with a woman named Detra Flame, who began the pilgrimage and carried it out for nearly thirty years. When she was fourteen years old, Flame lay deathly ill in the hospital and was visited several times by Valentino himself. He would bring Flame a red rose, and according to her obituary in the *New York Times*, said, "You're not going to die at all...you are going to live for many more years. But one thing for sure, if I die before you do, please come and stay by me because I don't want to be alone."

Flame was found dead in her home surrounded by Valentino memorabilia. She never married. Others have taken up this tradition over the years, and the summer of 2026 will mark the one hundredth anniversary of his death. We plan to pack our best black outfits and veils and head out to the Hollywood Forever Cemetery on that day. The cemetery also hosts movie showings, musical performances, and other events, so make sure to check out their calendar for tickets and information.

 Other horror icons buried in California include *Dracula* (1931) star Bela Lugosi at Holy Cross Cemetery in Culver City, and *Psycho* (1960) star Janet Leigh and Heather O'Rourke from *Poltergeist* (1982), both at Westwood Memorial Park in Los Angeles.

A Nightmare on Elm Street House
1428 NORTH GENESEE AVENUE, WEST HOLLYWOOD

In the heart of Hollywood's movie magic sits the house that served as the exterior shots for *A Nightmare on Elm Street* (1984). Director Wes Craven was inspired to write about the iconic character of Freddy Krueger, played by Robert Englund, after he read an article about a real occurrence happening in the United States. A large number of Hmong immigrants, fleeing from Laos after the Vietnam War, were dying in their sleep. Cultural beliefs led them to believe they were being sought by the Dab Tsong, a sleep demon. Medical experts concluded that the deaths were attributed to a combination of sudden unexplained nocturnal death syndrome (SUNDS) and cardiac arrhythmia, which were most prevalent among males from this specific area in Asia. Craven wondered what it would be like to explore the idea of a sleep demon (common among numerous cultures), sleep paralysis, and an entity that could kill people in their dreams.

The house most notably also was the home of the director Lorene Scafaria and her partner, Bo Burnham. The house went up for sale in the fall of 2021 and even held a special open house on Halloween for interested buyers. The house listing featured someone dressed as Freddy Krueger posing throughout the rooms and property as a cheeky nod to the house's iconic horror roots. When we visited in the fall of 2022, new owners were completing renovations on the property in the quaint neighborhood of Hollywood.

 Stop by the "murder house" from season one of *American Horror Story* (2011) at 1120 Westchester Place in Los Angeles. The house, built in 1902, was home to several families and even became a convent for nuns.

The Hollywood Sign

AT THE END OF MOUNT LEE DRIVE

The Hollywood sign, one of the most recognizable landmarks in the world, has always been a favorite of ours. Seeing the sign portrayed in numerous movies, television shows, and other media is a staple of our cultural zeitgeist and serves as an instant cue to establishing setting and general era. Originally built in 1923 as a temporary ad for a real estate development, the sign initially said "HOLLYWOODLAND" and was replaced in 1978 with the structure we see today. Although iconic, the sign itself has some haunted history.

We interviewed our friend, writer and actress Erin Carere, who experienced seeing a ghostly figure at a friend's Hollywood Hills home in 2010. While visiting one evening, Erin noticed a figure passing the living room window. Worried she had forgotten to close the gate to the property, she asked if she should go close it. Her friend Susan asked, "Did you see it?" The figure, Erin recalls, was dressed in a vintage outfit and emerged as a hazy, creamy color. She took a closer look out the window and noticed the living room sat on the hill, above a two-story drop. There

was no way someone could have been walking by! "That's the ghost," Susan replied calmly. After doing some further research on possible ghosts in the area, Erin concluded that it may be Peg Entwistle, who died by suicide in 1932 by jumping off the *H* in the Hollywood sign. At age twenty-four, Entwistle perceived her career as an actress had failed even though she had appeared in numerous plays and even a film by that point in her life. Others also believe Entwistle's ghost haunts the area, including joggers who report seeing a woman who fits her description, dressed in 1930s attire and smelling of gardenias, which was supposedly her favorite scent. She left a suicide note that read:

> *"I am afraid, I am a coward. I am sorry for everything. If I had done this a long time ago, it would have saved a lot of pain. P.E."*

If you are looking for a close-up view of the Hollywood sign, we recommend driving up through the Hollywood Hills and stopping at the dog park to admire the icon and spy some sweet pooches too.

 The Hollywood sign has been destroyed in horror movies, including *Escape from LA* (1996) and *Resident Evil: Afterlife* (2010).

The Pike

While in Long Beach, make sure to visit some notable locations like The Pike amusement park, which has a strange history all its own. While filming an episode of *The Six Million Dollar Man* (1973–1978), a prop master discovered that what he thought to be a wax mannequin actually contained the body of a human! Elmer McCurdy, a bank robber who was shot and killed by police, had been mummified in 1911. His body was put on public display in Oklahoma until 1916. For a nickel, patrons could view McCurdy, who was known as "The Bandit Who Wouldn't Give Up," and then became part of the traveling carnival circuit up until the 1960s. McCurdy's body changed ownership several times and ended up at The Pike. After its discovery during filming, his body was positively identified and buried in 1977 back in Oklahoma.

The Dark Art Emporium

While in Long Beach, also check out The Dark Art Emporium. According to the Visit Long Beach website, "The Dark Art Emporium is a diverse environment dedicated to showcasing the artists and creators that often fly under the radar of most people's perception of fine art. Here you will find everything from real human skulls, creepy dolls, unorthodox taxidermy, lowbrow and dark fine art. We specialize in the strange and unusual because we ourselves are the strange and unusual." Just three minutes away, you can eat at The 4th Horseman. The restaurant features pizzas with names like Rosemary's Baby and Slasher, so you know it's a must-stop and a must-eat.

The Hollywood Roosevelt
7000 HOLLYWOOD BOULEVARD

Located on Hollywood Boulevard, the Hollywood Roosevelt is arguably the most famous hotel in the heart of the action. And it just may be the most haunted. Built in 1926, the Hollywood Roosevelt has seen numerous celebrities stay under its roof, including Marilyn Monroe and Clark Gable, and was host to the very first Academy Awards ceremony. The property has numerous ghost stories tied to it, including the ghosts of actors Errol Flynn and Montgomery Clift haunting guests, and a little girl named Caroline, who appears in a blue dress and has been seen looking for her mother. Before we were aware of this legend, we wore matching blue dresses to attend Halloween Horror Nights as the Grady Girls from *The Shining* (1980). Little did we know, we were cosplaying as a resident ghost.

We appreciated not only the convenient location of the Roosevelt but the customer service, food options, and pool. We also were able to attend showings of multiple horror movies during our stay, including *Night of the Living Dead* (1963) in the Cinegrill Theater and *The Shining* (1980) poolside. Sitting under the palm trees and stars in Hollywood, watching one of our favorite movies, will be a memory we will always hold with us. The Roosevelt also offers rooftop yoga, massages, and other events to help you relax and enjoy your stay.

The Queen Mary

The *Queen Mary* in Long Beach, about twenty-five miles south of LA, may be one of the most iconic spots in California for hopeful ghost peepers to visit. Built in 1930, the *Queen Mary* was a legendary ocean liner that boasted not only famous guests like Clark Gable and Audrey Hepburn but is also known for numerous hauntings. The ship has been transformed into a hotel and is permanently docked in Long Beach.

According to the ship's ghost tour, one of the most haunted rooms is stateroom B340. Walter J. Adamson died in the room in 1948, and guests have since reported seeing a man at the foot of their bed, hearing knocks at the door, and witnessing the bathroom lights go on and off by themselves. Although we didn't stay overnight on the *Queen Mary*, we would recommend requesting this room for your future reservations. If you're not able to reserve that room, there are plenty of other haunted places to visit while on board. Ghostly wet footprints have been spotted near the first class swimming pool by guests over the years, and while that may not seem strange, it is when you consider the pool has not been open in decades. Other people have reported smelling cigars and perfume in the staterooms, hearing squeals and whistling in empty rooms, and feeling sudden temperature changes while on board. One ghost story includes a man who was crushed under a watertight door during a drill and now haunts the spot where he perished. Make sure to attend the ghost tour and enjoy the eerie lighting and sound effects they use to recreate what others have witnessed. On our various tours of the *Queen Mary*, we experienced floating orbs and strange blurring in our photos, cold spots, and unfamiliar feelings as we wandered the various decks and rooms open to us.

WHERE TO SHOP

Dark Delicacies, Bookstore

822 NORTH HOLLYWOOD WAY, BURBANK

An LA mainstay, Dark Delicacies is our home away from home. We've been lucky enough to do two book signings there and to have met both Del and Sue Howison, the fearless leaders of the best horror shop in Burbank and beyond. The couple founded Dark Delicacies in 1994, a lifetime ago for independent shops. As book lovers we're hypnotized by their selection, all horror, many signed editions. There are also countless horror collectibles, horror board games, and T-shirts unique to the shop. One of our prized possessions (we each have one) is a twenty-fifth-anniversary pin featuring Del and his trademark long white hair. He's an icon in the horror community, as he and his wife have created a friendly, welcoming atmosphere for both horror fans and horror creators. The event calendar is filled with visits from authors and filmmakers, as well as extra-special events like their *My Bloody Valentine* (1981) book and board game launch in February, with cast members of the original film and game creators in attendance. If you go to only one place in LA for your horror fix, stop by Dark Delicacies, and tell Del and Sue we sent you.

> ➤ Numerous television shows and films have featured the *Queen Mary*, including *The X-Files* (1993–2018) episode "Triangle," *The Poseidon Adventure* (1972), and episodes of *Murder, She Wrote* (1984–1996).

The exterior of the house used in the television show *Dexter* (2006–2013) is located in Long Beach, and, fun fact, Meg named her second son after the title character!

Unique Vintage, Clothing Shop

212 NORTH SAN FERNANDO BOULEVARD, BURBANK

If you're a goth enthusiast, you've no doubt shopped online at Unique Vintage. While it's fun to peruse the photos and reviews via your phone or computer, it's so much more enjoyable to visit the shop in person while in Burbank and try on all of your favorite pieces. The shop began in 2000 when CEO and founder Katie Echeverry sought out and resold vintage items. A few years later, she began to design and sell her own vintage-inspired creations. This female-owned company is diverse and body inclusive, and has lots of horror-themed items that we love. From dresses and rompers to accessories like earrings and handbags, we have purchased numerous items from the shop over the years. Maybe we should invest in some stock.

Halloween Town, Horror Shop

2921 WEST MAGNOLIA BOULEVARD, BURBANK

If we had brought large empty suitcases with us to California, we would have filled them with merchandise from Halloween Town in Burbank. Like a horror fan's fever dream, the store has every decoration, costume, and collectible that you can imagine from your favorite horror franchises. We walked around wide-eyed like children in a candy store, moving from one room to another with awe and delight. With over twenty years in business, Halloween Town boasts three huge stores only six doors apart.

While we visited in the month of October, the stores were extra busy, so make sure to allow more time to pick out the perfect props, wigs, or books to take home with you. We love our own seasonal Spirit Halloween stores but are jealous that a year-round store like Halloween Town exists. Or perhaps it's meant to be; otherwise, we would surely be broke by now.

WHERE TO EAT

Mel's Drive-In

1660 NORTH HIGHLAND AVENUE

With several locations throughout California, Mel's Drive-In is a fun, nostalgic stop for a meal. The Hollywood Mel's is located in the historic Max Factor building and shares a space with the Hollywood Museum. We enjoyed burgers and fries before ending our meal with spiked milkshakes. After a meal, pop over to the museum, where you'll see the Dungeon of Doom exhibit featuring the jail cell and other props and costumes from *The Silence of the Lambs* (1990), *The Walking Dead* (2010–2022), and more.

The Breakfast Club LA

1600 VINE STREET, HOLLYWOOD

When looking for a fun restaurant close to our hotel, we discovered The Breakfast Club LA. While colorful and self-proclaimedly "Instagrammable," it may not be an obvious choice for those of us who like to dress in all black, but the fun atmosphere, impeccable service, and delicious food made us immediate fans. Serving everything from coffee to cocktails, this spot offers breakfast all day long. We had fluffy waffles with fresh strawberries and a vegan platter, and will definitely be visiting again.

Casa Vega

13301 VENTURA BOULEVARD, SHERMAN OAKS

A Los Angeles staple for nearly seventy years, Casa Vega offers authentic Mexican food in the San Fernando Valley. We met a friend for lunch and were seated in the cozy outdoor area, where we enjoyed margaritas, chips and salsa, and other Mexican favorites. As one of Los Angeles's longest-running family-owned restaurants, Casa Vega has been a place to spot celebrities from as far back as Cary Grant in the 1960s to the filming of *Once Upon a Time in Hollywood* (2019). Enjoy drinks at the historic bar, which features fresh squeezed juices and numerous options for wines, cocktails, and beers.

The Cauldron Spirits & Brews

8028 BEACH BOULEVARD, BUENA PARK

If you're looking for a gothic, witchy-themed place to grab a bite or a drink, stop by the Cauldron Spirits & Brews in Buena Park, California. The restaurant features "Witch Wine?" Sundays, with half-price bottles of wine and craft cocktails that "evoke the magical aura of alchemy, witchcraft, and enchanted brews." The Cauldron had us at *hello* with its seating, decor, and book displays. Settle in and enjoy the spooky surroundings while sipping on a Cthulhu's Revenge or Bourbon and Brimstone.

A WOMAN YOU SHOULD KNOW

Maila Nurmi (Vampira)

1922–2008

While most horror fans will recognize Vampira, they may not be aware of her story and history. Maila Nurmi, a Finnish American born in 1922, is a horror icon, trendsetter, and beloved actress. Nurmi moved to New York City in the early 1940s, where it's reported she was fired from a Broadway play by Mae West, who feared Nurmi was upstaging her. Nurmi gained notoriety in New York afterward when she appeared in a horror-themed show where she lay in a coffin, walked around a cemetery set, and let out a bloodcurdling scream. While at a costume party years later in Los Angeles, Nurmi dressed as Morticia from *The Addams Family* cartoons, first published in 1937, and caught the attention of a television producer. She starred in *The Vampira Show* from 1954 to 1955 and appeared in only twenty more movies and television shows, many of them uncredited, before her death in 2008. Nurmi was the first horror hostess in history and will live on as one of the original goth girls forever.

TRAVEL TIPS

1. Unless you're comfortable driving in a lot of traffic, consider taking rideshares while in Los Angeles. The freeways can be intimidating to those not used to them and potentially stressful. We've driven our own cars, rented, and taken rideshares on our multiple trips to the city, and have decided we prefer that someone else drive. Plus, you'll be able to look out the window and admire the scenery and may even recognize multiple filming locations on your travels.

2. Changing time zones can be a big difference for anyone traveling from far away, but even if you're coming from the central time zone, it can be jarring to not find coffee immediately in the morning (especially for Meg!). Check the times of when shops open and plan ahead for your day. We discovered that coffee wasn't available until 8 a.m. at the Starbucks across the street, and many shops didn't open until 10 a.m.

3. You can plan ahead to see celebrities while in Los Angeles by looking at theater and television show websites to secure tickets and save your spot at premieres. We saw the red-carpet entrance for *Halloween Kills* (2021) at the TCL Chinese Theatre and got tickets to multiple talk shows where some of our favorite writers and actors were appearing.

4. Los Angeles and the surrounding communities are not as walkable as you may perceive. A mile in New York City is not the same in California. Be safe and don't walk in areas that may cross busy

traffic. We learned the hard way by trying to walk from one store to another one day and soon realized we'd be crossing multiple bridges, intersections, and various neighborhoods that weren't necessarily pedestrian friendly. Our rideshare driver got a chuckle over our naivety, and we enjoyed a short, relaxing ride to our next destination.

5. Don't be like Meg and get all dressed up like a Grady Girl, show up to Universal Studios Halloween Horror Nights stand in a long line, and give them your tickets only to discover you bought tickets for Universal Florida...and then get sent to another line and have to pay again. Learn from Meg's mistakes.

OTHER SPOOKY PLACES IN CALIFORNIA

A Donner Party Trip

LAKE TAHOE

Ever since Jack Torrance brought up the Donner Party at the beginning of *The Shining* (1980), we've been curious about this true tragedy. Meg watched a documentary on the ill-fated trip as a teen and highly recommends the book *The Indifferent Stars Above: The Harrowing Saga of the Donner Party* (2015) by Daniel James Brown. It is an unflinching look at the missteps that led to the death of dozens of pioneers in the Sierra Nevada mountains. Of course, it is the desperation leading to cannibalism that has remained as the most-talked-about aspect of that winter of 1846. What struck Meg in this in-depth account was the particular cruelty the women faced, as mothers starved so that their children could eat, as well as remaining the voice of reason when all men had abandoned camp. A few years ago, her husband suggested Meg tag along to a work conference of his near Lake Tahoe, California. Meg immediately jumped on her laptop and brought up the Google Map of the resort, because she wanted to see if she'd be able to do some Donner tourism. Sure enough, the memorial and museum were nearby. Yes, she agreed to go. As long as he accompanied her to this monument to the fallen pioneers.

Nestled in the Sierra Nevadas in Truckee, California, is the impressive statue placed where one of the party had built a cabin. It is something to behold, the figure of a man, woman, and child with this beneath: "Virile to risk and find, kindly withal and a ready help. Facing the brunt of fate, indomitable, unafraid."

This "brunt of fate" is on display in the museum steps away. Opened in 2015, it has artifacts from the Donner Party, personal belongings like combs and wallets, along with a comprehensive look at the lives touched by the brutal weather of 1846. There are other exhibits, too, like the history of the Chinese railroad workers that echoes the experience we learned about coming up in our chapter on Portland, Oregon.

Visiting this part of the world is perfect for nature lovers. Meg and her husband enjoyed rafting on the Tahoe River and hiking the many trails, though it's the Donner monument and museum that linger in her memory, a haunting visit that made her appreciate the narrative of America's early pioneers, especially the women.

A Quick Castle Stop in Napa

CALISTOGA

What's more gothic than a castle? Good news! You don't have to go to Europe to stand upon the stoned battlements, pretending you're a Transylvanian queen looking down upon the peasants. In Calistoga, the heart of the Napa wine haven, is Castello di Amorosa, the castle and winery of a wealthy Europe-loving American.

On the guided tour, we learned just how fastidious winemaker Dario Sattui was in the painstaking reconstruction of a thirteenth-century Italian castle: "In my mind, everything had to be authentic, or it wouldn't be worth the effort. Faking it in any way might be all right for others, but I would know the difference, making it a failed attempt to explore my passion for medieval architecture... You simply can't build an 'old structure' using modern techniques and tools. It would look fake, and everyone would realize it's an imitation. Rather, we were going to build the structure—within the limits of the current building code—using the same techniques medieval builders had relied on eight hundred years ago." His commitment to detail is staggering, in the authentic materials from Italy, from the floors to the furniture. One hundred and seven rooms span multiple floors, including underground crypts filled with barrels of wine. So, it's basically paradise. There are winding staircases, a chapel, a drawbridge, and thankfully some bathrooms, because the thirteenth century wasn't perfect. And don't forget to take photos in the "torture chamber," where Sattui has assembled a collection of medieval torture devices that look like something out of a Vincent Price/Roger Corman picture.

The Winchester Mystery House

SAN JOSE

The Winchester Mystery House is one of the most famous haunted places in the state. Having celebrated its one hundredth anniversary in 2023, the Winchester is described as "the world's most unusual and sprawling mansion, featuring twenty-four thousand square feet, ten thousand windows, two thousand doors, one hundred sixty rooms, fifty-two skylights, forty-seven stairways and fireplaces, seventeen chimneys, thirteen bathrooms, and six kitchens." The mansion is known to be a haunted destination that has been written about and explored by various horror enthusiasts.

Hotel del Coronado

SAN DIEGO

If traveling to San Diego, California, make sure to book a room at the Hotel del Coronado. Built in 1888, the hotel has been purportedly haunted by a ghost for over a century. In 1892, twenty-four-year-old Kate Morgan checked into the hotel alone to meet up with a lover. After five days, when he didn't show up, she took her own life and is said to have never left. Guests have reported flickering lights, strange scents and sounds, and temperature changes while visiting the property, and Kate's third-floor room is highly sought after by paranormal enthusiasts.

WELCOME TO

MARIETTA

EORGIA

POPULATION: 61,497

SPOOKIEST THING TO HAPPEN HERE

The Okefenokee Swamp in Georgia is home to rumored creatures. In 1829, people started to talk about a "swamp thing" lurking in the murky water. It was reported in a local newspaper that nine hunters ventured out in search of the creature, but only four returned after being attacked by the beast. Survivors reported the monster's tracks to be over nineteen inches long and nine inches wide, and said the creature itself stood over thirteen feet tall. Because of how long ago this incident took place, it's difficult to verify. There are more recent reports of creatures in the swamp, too. In 2007 a man reported he saw an animal he described as part bear and part primate: "It almost moved like a spider, using all fours, but not like a horse would. It was right up on the edge of the creek looking at us."

The swamp is also home to an estimated ten thousand to thirteen thousand gators. Be careful out there, friends. One of our favorite *The X-Files* (1993–2018) episodes, entitled "Quagmire," takes place in the Okefenokee Swamp. Spoiler alert: Scully's (Gillian Anderson's) beloved dog, Queequeg, meets his demise while the agents are on search for a creature called Big Blue. RIP, king.

HIDDEN GEM WE DISCOVERED

Earl and Rachel Smith Strand Theatre

117 NORTH PARK SQUARE

The Renegade Film Festival, originally The Women in Horror Film Festival, is held annually at the Earl and Rachel Smith Strand Theatre in Marietta. The gorgeous historic theater was built in 1935 and currently hosts concerts, comedy shows, and the showing of classic films. Stop by to see the venue and meet fellow horror fans and filmmakers at the festival. Renegade's website states, "The Renegade Film Festival is built on elevating marginalized voices. We are proud to showcase diverse content and promote inclusion and visibility in order to bring balance and equality to independent cinema." The festival awards trophies coined "The Lizzies," which feature a hand wearing blood red nails, holding an ax, Lizzie Borden style. We've had the opportunity to meet filmmakers, writers, and crew members behind amazing horror films when we've attended the festival over the past several years, and we encourage others to partake.

The first year the festival was held, we stayed at the Crowne Plaza in Peachtree City and felt as if we were at summer camp. The wooded surroundings and trails gave us a sense of escape while we were still very near Atlanta. Enjoying lunch on our first day in the hotel restaurant, we overlooked a pond on the property with a sprinkler protruding out of the water. Being in the horror spirit, we fully expected Jason Voorhees to emerge *Friday the 13th* (1980) style out of the water and amble toward us. It didn't happen, but a girl can dream.

MOST FAMOUS TRUE CRIME

One of Georgia's most prolific murderers was known as "The Casanova Killer." Officially, Paul John Knowles was tied to the death of eighteen people, but he confessed to another seventeen murders that could not be proven. All of his confirmed murders took place between July and November 1974 in Georgia and Florida. He was captured at a roadblock, sent to prison, escaped, and was shot and killed shortly thereafter.

SPOOKY MOVIES AND BOOKS SET HERE

BOOKS

The House Next Door (1978) by
    Anne Rivers Siddons
Those Bones Are Not My Child
    (1999) by Toni Cade Bambara
Such a Pretty Smile (2022) by
    Kristi DeMeester

MOVIES

Cape Fear (1962)
Squirm (1976)
Cocaine Bear (2023)

 Camp Daniel Morgan in Rutledge, Georgia, is the perfect stop for horror fans because two iconic movies were filmed there: *Friday the 13th Part VI: Jason Lives* (1986) and *Fear Street Part 2: 1978* (2021).

WHAT TO DO

Kennesaw House

1 DEPOT STREET

Built in the 1840s as a cotton warehouse, the Kennesaw House turned into a restaurant, then an inn in 1855. Because of its proximity to the railroad tracks, many soldiers and spies stayed on the premises during the Civil War. The building next door became a makeshift hospital and morgue, and ghostly activity has been reported ever since. Now home to the Marietta History Center, the Kennesaw House is one of the oldest buildings in the city, reported to be the home to over seven hundred restless spirits. One group of visitors reported riding in the elevator, and when the doors opened, they were in the basement amid a bustling hospital setting. They thought they had stumbled upon a Civil War reenactment, but when they asked the museum staff about it, they said they knew nothing of the kind.

Lake Lanier

1050 BUFORD DAM ROAD, BUFORD

When we began asking around about the most haunted places near Marietta, we were surprised to hear that a lake topped the list. But once we heard the story of Lake Lanier, about ninety minutes from Marietta, we nodded knowingly. Yep, sounds haunted to us.

Because of an act of Congress in 1946, the government began expanding waterways in the U.S. by creating human-made lakes. Meg lives in the one county of Minnesota that doesn't have a natural lake, so she's grateful for the few created lakes—also doubly grateful after hearing about the origin of Lake Lanier. Since its creation in the mid-1950s, *seven hundred people* have died in and around the lake, including twenty-seven missing persons. Gulp. Those are staggering numbers that we have to break down. During the lake's creation, two hundred and fifty families were displaced, and twenty cemeteries were "moved." We think we know where this is going... Often when officials say a cemetery is moved, especially back in the day, they mean the gravestones were moved and not necessarily any of the bodies. Double gulp.

But wait—it gets worse: "Many of the structures, buildings, and roads that were flooded during the lake's creation were left as is. Divers find eerie relics of streets, walls, and houses intact like an abandoned ghost town on the lake's bottom. Discovery Channel's show *Expedition X* proved (to the extent they can 'prove' something) that there are twenty cemeteries with headstones and graves still at the bottom of the lake that were never removed. The ancestors of the disrupted populations were never relocated, thus sparking many stories of haunted encounters."

Lake Lanier is intended for recreation, yet the bottom of it is considered the most dangerous underwater surface in the United States. This is because of the debris like cars, bridges, and concrete buildings under the water instead of a nice sandy bottom. Debris is believed to be a factor in hundreds of boating accidents, as well as the reason the search for missing persons in the depths is so difficult. All of this is why we recommend staying out of Lake Lanier and instead taking a nice stroll beside it—maybe a goth picnic? Black tablecloth, blood red wine in studded goblets, you get the idea.

If you're searching for ghosts, people have reported seeing the frightening likeness of Susie Roberts, who died when her car fell off a bridge into Lake Lanier in 1958. She appears near the water in the blue dress she died in, missing her hands just as her body mysteriously was. Lake visitors have also reported hearing disturbing moans from the water, as well as a male ghost who carries a lantern.

Brave enough to dip your toe in Lake Lanier? If you don't see the ghosts or get scraped by debris, another reason to enjoy the area is that the lake has been used in filming several scenes for Netflix's crime drama *Ozark* (2017–2022).

Ghosts of Marietta Tour
VARIOUS MEETING LOCATIONS

When you visit Marietta, you can choose from a number of tours, including walking, trolley, and self-guided. Wear comfortable shoes and listen to spooky stories based on history, documented sightings, and firsthand accounts. We caught ourselves looking over our shoulders more than once as we heard tales of the spirits who have never left Marietta, like Catherine, well known by locals as a ghost who shows herself time and time again.

Catherine frequents the Marietta-Cobb Museum, which houses nineteenth- and twentieth-century American art in a Classical Revival with impressive columns. The good news: Catherine is more on the playful spectrum of ghosts, not considered to be frightening at all. After the tour, we'll never view the buildings the same again after considering their history and the people who once lived and shopped there. Unlike tours in some other cities, the Marietta ghost tours run year-round but only on the weekends. Book your tickets in advance to experience a frightfully good time.

The Statue of Mary Meinert

161 CHURCH STREET

Located in the St. James Episcopal Cemetery, the statue of Mary Meinert—a woman holding two infants in her arms—is difficult to miss. The story behind her death may explain why some claim to hear her weeping and see tears falling from her eyes.

Mary died in 1898 at age thirty-four from tuberculosis when her infant twin daughters were only a month old. She left behind four other children and her husband. Although local lore claims you can circle her statue at night and her ghost will appear, we recommend not taunting any spirits. And please, no trespassing. Visit Mary during the day and see if you notice her twins switch places, as some claim to have witnessed. Notably, this cemetery is also the resting place of JonBenet Ramsey, who was murdered in 1996.

The Walking Dead Tours

SENOIA, GEORGIA

Having loved *The Walking Dead* (2010–2022) since its premiere, we were thrilled to travel to Georgia together to meet fellow fans. As frequent booksellers at Walker Stalker Conventions, we'd come to know how friendly *Walking Dead* fans truly are. We've even been able to spy a few of the actors at the conventions over the years, like Norman Reedus, who plays Daryl, and Tom Payne, who played Jesus.

If you're looking for an incredible experience, head about an hour south of Marietta to Senoia, Georgia, for several tour options of sites featured on the show. Through Georgia Tour Company, you can choose self-guided, walking, golf cart, or van tours that will bring you through multiple locations. These include the streets of Alexandria, houses built for the TV show that honestly look nice enough and real enough to move into. There are also more rugged locations, like the Commonwealth gate, rusted to apocalyptic perfection. If you're lucky, you'll see the pudding house (if you know, you know) as well as Negan's prezombie house. Walking tours are around two hours long, while van tours last five hours and include lunch. Knowledgeable guides will take you through plenty of places you'll recognize from seasons three through the end of the series and show you sights along the way. If you want to see absolutely everything, plan to spend a few days in Senoia, since the five-hour tour options can't be combined due to distance and time.

After you've spent a full day pretending to live in a postapocalyptic zombie hellscape, do what the characters of *The Walking Dead* can't do: stuff your face with lots of food. The perfect place? Nic and Norman's, owned by Greg Nicotero (producer of *The Walking Dead,* as well as head of the incredibly disgusting makeup effects) and Norman Reedus. Their restaurant serves up lots of meat, as well as Norman's Pick, a plant-based patty with beets and a fried egg that's so yummy it could turn anyone into a vegetarian. And you know we love cocktails with cheeky names, so you *have* to order a Bloody Nicotero, which promises hot sauce and a bloody eyeball.

Stranger Things Filming Locations

Another one of our favorite shows, *Stranger Things* (2016–), is filmed in Georgia, and we are obsessed with getting a glimpse of any place where the action has taken place. Again, through Georgia Tour Company, you can book five-hour van tours that will take you to places like the fictional Hawkins High School and the location of Will's funeral, as well as optional add-ons, like visiting Hopper's cabin or attempting to get out of an Upside Down escape room. You can also build your own tour, thanks to *Atlanta Magazine,* which has compiled a map of all the best filming locations. Perhaps you can go total *Stranger Things*, jump on bikes with friends, and make the trek. Have dinner at Enzo's, where Judith stood up Hopper on their first date (aww, poor guy). It's actually called Dominick's Italian of Historic Norcross. If you're still hungry after all that pasta, head to Tiffany's Kitchen, known as Benny's Burgers on the show. This is the diner that Eleven runs to in the first episode after escaping Hawkins Lab. Just like her, you can stuff a cheeseburger in your mouth super fast before you get back on your bike. Next stop could be to shop at Starcourt Mall, actually the Gwinnett Place Mall in Duluth, Georgia, the main setting in season three, where Steve and Robin scooped ice cream and Eleven bought that psychedelic blouse that is so '80s our eyes hurt. Warning: the Gwinnett Place Mall doesn't have as much neon lighting and teased hair as Starcourt Mall would have you believe. While the series wrapped filming in 2024, we look forward to the other iterations that the creators are championing for the future, which means many more locations to visit in the Marietta area.

The Gone with the Wind Museum

472 POWDER SPRINGS STREET

Before we tell you about this beautifully curated collection, it's vital we recognize the problematic nature of both the 1936 book by Margaret Mitchell and the 1939 film. Products of their time, both versions have egregiously racist portrayals of the antebellum South. While the film is a watershed moment in epic cinema, and it provided the first Oscar to a Black actor (Hattie McDaniel won for her role as Mammy), its controversy is justified.

That said, we both grew up watching the film. Meg read the thick paperback in high school, spending her entire holiday break caught up in the world of tempestuous Scarlett O'Hara. What is more gothic than when Scarlett is in the crumbling Tara, once a luxurious mansion, wearing a dress made out of her drapes? Well, maybe her love-hate relationship with handsome scoundrel Rhett Butler.

It was an overcast morning when we made our short walk from the Hilton Atlanta/Marietta hotel to the museum, curious to see what goodies they might have.

Housed in Brumby Hall, a traditional southern mansion built in 1851 that Scarlett O'Hara would feel at home in, the museum hosts many exhibits, including a new selection of artifacts from the film. For ten bucks you can see art, props, and, best of all, a slice of filmic history. Our favorite displays were the costumes. The dresses from the film are iconic to say the least, their grandeur even more awesome in person. We had the museum to ourselves that morning, with a knowledgeable host who gave us a tour of the many items, including letters of Margaret Mitchell and film call sheets. The gift shop, which is free to visit, has every book devoted to *Gone with the Wind* you could think of, including *The Road to Tara: The Life of Margaret Mitchell* (2014). I picked up a copy, and we both filled our bags with gifts for friends. Meg's older brother instilled a love of *Gone with the Wind* in her, as well as pretty much anything played on Turner Classic Movies. So, we made sure to get him an art print of that forest-green "drapes dress."

 Oakland Cemetery in Atlanta, whose history dates back to 1850, is a popular stop for goths visiting Georgia. According to *Atlanta Ghosts,* "The first Atlanta resident to be buried at the cemetery was a doctor by the name of James Nissen. According to legend, Dr. Nissen harbored a crippling fear of being buried alive. To alleviate his fears, the anxious doctor requested that his jugular vein be severed prior to his burial. His request was obliged, ensuring Nissen would never wake up on the wrong side of the grave." Yikes. Other notable people buried there include Selena Sloan Butler, who founded the nation's first parent-teacher association for African Americans in Atlanta in 1911, and renowned author Margaret Mitchell.

Monster Mini Golf

2505 CHASTAIN MEADOWS PARKWAY NW

Monster Mini Golf—inside, so you don't have to worry about the Georgia heat—is the perfectly dark, spooky, and air-conditioned place where goths like us can chill. Instead of recognizable Universal monsters, the creatures here are unique to the mini golf course. Kind of like if Chuck E. Cheese and his friends were skeletons, ogres, and fog-spitting trees. Watch for special events like glow-in-the-dark night golf and special weekend deals.

If aliens are more your thing, may we suggest Cosmic Mini Golf and Play in nearby Kennesaw. Again, you can stay cool indoors, this time in the vastness of space. Cute extraterrestrials beckon you in to play the neon course. And it's so dark no one will see when you hit a spaceship instead of getting a hole in one.

 There are numerous horror conventions and film festivals held throughout the state of Georgia, including the aforementioned Renegade Film Festival, the Atlanta Horror Film Festival, the Southern Horror Film Festival, and the Buried Alive Film Festival, as well as the Georgia Pop and Horror Con, and the Savannah Horror Fest. Watch horror films, meet celebrities, and have a blast.

WHERE TO STAY

The Hilton Atlanta/Marietta

500 POWDER SPRINGS STREET

The Hilton Atlanta/Marietta Hotel and Conference Center is not only a convenient place to stay, it also has major *The Shining* (1980) vibes. Located next to the *Gone with the Wind* Museum, the Hilton was built on the former grounds of the Georgia Military Institute. In the hotel restaurant, we witnessed rocking chairs on the porch moving on their own (maybe because of the wind?) and knew this location was our jam. The rooms are comfortable, food and drink are available on site, and parking is plentiful. We enjoyed touring the historical photos and artifacts on premises, and imbibed in the local craft brews the hotel bar offered. Enjoy the gorgeous views of the golf course on the property, and bask in the sun next to the outdoor pool. Some guests claim to have heard strange noises in the hallways they attributed to the ghosts from the former military institute.

The Stanley House

236 CHURCH STREET

If you prefer a more historic, cozy atmosphere for your stay in Marietta, consider booking a room at the Stanley House. Established in 1895, this bed-and-breakfast served as the summer residence of President Woodrow Wilson's aunt and uncle. Every room features a king-size bed and private bathroom, with gourmet continental breakfast on the weekdays and hot plated southern breakfast on the weekends. The convenient location, just three blocks from Marietta Square, makes this a great choice for a place to stay.

Marietta Square Farmers Market

68 NORTH MARIETTA PARKWAY NW

Although this farmers market exists, we were tricked into thinking a different market was set up in Marietta Square one day. As we began browsing through the booths, we noticed a sign warning passersby of filming taking place in the area. We later found out a movie starring Chris Evans had set up to commence shooting. We quickly exited the area but kept an eye out the window as we enjoyed brunch in the square. The farmers market, which is open from 9 a.m. to noon year-round on Saturdays, features an average of fifty-four vendors selling fresh Georgia-grown produce, soaps, honey, and preserves.

 For a truly unique experience, venture to Doll's Head Trail in Atlanta, a less than two-mile round-trip hike with a found-objects art display. Be aware of snakes on the trail, and only contribute to the art with objects you find along the way.

Antique Shopping

MARIETTA SQUARE

One of our favorite things to do when traveling is to stop by local antique shops and see all the treasures they hold. Marietta has several fun places to discover unique finds, such as Antiques on the Square and Park West

Vintage, and we left with more than we intended. What else is new? From vintage jewelry to creepy dolls, the antique shops in Marietta contained so many rare items, and browsing was a fun way to spend an entire afternoon.

Bookmiser, Bookstore

3822 ROSWELL ROAD, #117

If you know us, you know we're always looking for a fun local bookstore. Bookmiser, established in 1998, has an incredible story of how they started while brainstorming on a family road trip. According to their website, "We all agreed there was no such thing as a 'bad' used bookstore. However, we wanted to be different, unique, and create a concept that would separate us from others in the industry. Our bookstore would be clean and organized, not dusty, musty, and in disarray; the store would be easy to see, easy to find, easy to access; our trade and pricing concept would be simple, keeping rules to a minimum; the inventory would be clean and of high quality; the bookstore experience would include more than books, featuring music of decades gone by—the '30s, '40s, and '50s." The bookstore not only has a great selection of books but also hosts numerous virtual and in-person book events.

Scull Shoals Ruins is a must-see for those road-tripping through Georgia. Located in the heart of the Oconee National Forest in Greene County, this ghost town was once a frontier village in the 1700s. After a flood in the 1880s, the town was destroyed and eventually abandoned.

WHERE TO EAT

WR Social House

25 NORTH PARK SQUARE

For brunch and mimosas, we stopped at WR Social House in Marietta Square. At this locally owned restaurant with fresh ingredients, we enjoyed delicious food in the bustling atmosphere while we planned our shopping excursions for the day.

Red Hare Brewing and Distilling

29 WEST PARK SQUARE

A short walk from Marietta Square, Red Hare Brewing and Distilling offers several core brands on tap as well as seasonal and small-batch liquors to try. The indoor and outdoor seating provided a nice vibe for visiting with fellow creatives. With a variety of menu options and entertainment, Red Hare is a great spot for a night out.

L on North

113 NORTH PARK SQUARE

Looking for local, handmade food that's free of any artificial flavors and preservatives? Stop by L on North in Marietta Square, which has everything from salads and sandwiches to pizzas and tacos. We enjoyed drinks and food at L on North more than once while visiting Marietta. For a special dessert treat, try the fried chocolate cake or the cheesecake empanada.

Curious about Georgia cryptids? Travel to the Expedition: Bigfoot exhibit, located in Blue Ridge. The museum is considered North Georgia's "biggest" family attraction and features 3,700 square feet of self-guided exhibits.

A WOMAN YOU SHOULD KNOW

Vanessa Ionta Wright

(1976–)

Filmmaker and Renegade Film Festival director Vanessa Ionta Wright is a lifelong horror fan who started the festival in Georgia in 2017. Her goal is to highlight diverse voices, particularly female-identifying people in the horror genre, to promote inclusion and equality on screen and behind the scenes.

Graduating from Ohio University with a degree in video production and film, Vanessa had the opportunity to direct an adaptation of Stephen King's story "Rainy Season." As the writer, director, and executive producer of the film, she said she was drawn to the story by the overwhelming sense of dread and desperation. With more festivals and films under her belt since then, Vanessa is a woman to know and one to watch in the Georgia film scene and beyond.

TRAVEL TIPS

1. Atlanta, Georgia, twenty miles south of Marietta, has the busiest airport in the world, serving over one hundred million passengers per year. Allow extra time to get through security, and then enjoy the permanent and rotating art exhibits on display in the airport before your flight.

2. Ghost tours are available year-round in Marietta but mainly on the weekends, so make sure to check schedules online and book ahead of time. Several other cities offer ghost tours in Georgia, including Atlanta, Savannah, and Roswell.

3. While so many television shows and movies are being filmed in the state of Georgia, it's important to remember to respect sets, boundaries, and spoilers for anything you may see in person. Look for signage where productions are filming, and be aware that you may appear on film if you are in the area. If you haven't been on the set of a television show or movie, we highly recommend it to see the process and the work that goes into it and to potentially spot yourself on-screen.

4. If you're comfortable driving, we recommend renting a car to get the most bang for your buck in the state of Georgia. You'll be able to plan your route, schedule tours and stays, and come and go as you please while visiting. Road-tripping to Georgia? Even better. Refer to other chapters in *Travels of Terror* and see how to best utilize your vacation time by making other spooky stops along the way.

5. Check out all Georgia has to offer; there are places that would surprise you, such as the Chattahoochee Bamboo Forest as well as Providence Canyon State Park, known as "Georgia's Little Grand Canyon."

POPULATION: 641,162

SPOOKIEST THING TO HAPPEN HERE

On the outskirts of Portland sits the "Witch's House," a crumbling edifice of a stone mansion, threaded through with greenery. It is exactly what you might expect to find if you went searching in the woods for the Blair Witch. The long-neglected house has been rife with rumor and legend, most predominantly by the true tale of Anna Balch.

In the 1800s, Balch fell in love with a man who her father disapproved of. As soon as the young couple came back to Portland after their elopement, Balch's father killed her new husband. Devastated by both her husband's death and her father's execution for the murder, Anna Balch was sent to marry another man she didn't love. She ended up outliving her next two husbands, having nine healthy children, and owning two beautiful homes. As local Sarah Gilbert told us, "While it is said she died in 1922, there is not a gravestone , death certificate, or official record of her death. We believe Anna is the witch of the Witch's House, taking back power for young women from the patriarchy that would wrest it away."

If you visit the crumbled manse in Forest Park, let us know if you bump into the immortal witch Anna Balch.

HIDDEN GEM WE DISCOVERED

The Quality Bar

931 SOUTHWEST OAK STREET

On a whim, we popped into The Quality Bar in downtown Portland for a drink and slice of pizza and were pleasantly surprised to be greeted by horror art on the wall! Another surprise was using "The Magic Box" vending machine inside, which dispenses a grab bag of fun items with a nostalgic theme. We opted for one featuring 1990s items, which included random photos, a classic troll doll we coined "Bebe," heart-shaped sunglasses, hot-pink fingerless gloves, and jelly bracelets, just to name a few. We highly recommend this fun vending machine if you see one while out and about.

MOST FAMOUS TRUE CRIME

Serial killer Randall Woodfield, the "I–5 Killer," was a former student at Portland University. His first victims were in Portland, though as his moniker suggests, his killing spree took him all along Interstate 5, from California to Washington. If you're intrigued by Oregon crime, check out the podcast *Murder in the Rain*, or attend the Pacific Northwest True Crime Fest, which covers murder and mayhem throughout Oregon and Washington.

 # SPOOKY MOVIES AND BOOKS SET HERE

BOOKS

One Flew Over the Cuckoo's Nest (1962) by Ken Kesey

Everville (1994) by Clive Barker

Heartsick (2007) by Chelsea Cain

MOVIES

The Shining (1980)

Halloween Town (1998)

Coraline (2009)

The Mortuary Collection (2019)

 Much of the movie *Twilight* (2008) was filmed in Portland, Oregon, including the iconic Cullen house featured in the movie.

WHAT TO DO

Lone Fir Cemetery Tour

649 SOUTHEAST TWENTY-SIXTH AVENUE

For our historical ghost tour of Lone Fir Cemetery, we were instructed to meet our guides at Revolution Hall. Formerly a school, Revolution Hall is now a music and event venue. As we waited, we were pleased to find out there was a dog park adjacent. Cute dogs frolicked in the drizzle, unaware that we were there to go on a tour about death and tragedy...

Adorable doggies aside, Sarah Gilbert and her tour-guide apprentice, Edwin, met us for what ended up being a private tour. If you like having the experts all to yourself, then we recommend traveling to cold places in the winter.

It was evident right from the start that Sarah was extremely knowledgeable about not only Portland's history but the entirety of Oregon. She began with a talk on the millennium-long geological changes of the state before focusing on the Indigenous people and, finally, on the infamous Oregon Trail (we played that computer game HARD). We asked Sarah why goths would want to travel to Portland. "At first, this is a place where the shadow self is not just accepted but celebrated; theories that the Pacific Northwest's ruling planet is Pluto are just one aspect of the region's comfort with exploring darkness, both physical darkness and spirituality. The winters include many days that are very short, and the sun never comes out behind the clouds; fog is common every time of year; forests are thick and contain a substantial amount of the energy of decay and death, with life all around it. Sixteen-million-year-old basalt walls carry both sharp intensity and energy from a time of explosive change. Psychics, tarot readers, metal bands, psychedelic mushrooms, dripping mossy walls, anarchist mutual aid groups, Doc Marten stores, forests draped with lichen named for witch's hair and frog's skins—we have it all!"

We're definitely convinced.

As we walked along the residential streets toward the cemetery, Sarah stopped us in front of a palatial mansion with a wraparound porch. A classic Queen Anne, it was adorned with gothic gingerbread trim, the sort of house we could see ourselves living in as tragic poets in the Victorian era.

Sarah began to tell us about the house's first owner, William D. Fenton (long story short: Fenton was known for good things, like helping set up the Oregon Historical Society, but also bad things, like being a racist), and as we then started to discuss the importance of focusing on women and BIPOC in history, the current owner of the William D. Fenton House overheard us from the lawn. His two dogs (so many dog sightings in pet-friendly Portland) were taking care of business as he came over to say hello. He told us about how he had recently bought the property and was in the middle of restoring it. In fact, he'd come across some strange finds in the walls of the mansion, like a bottle of beer made with slightly less alcohol for nursing mothers! Ah...the good ol' days.

He also, quite casually, mentioned how he and his partner had witnessed ghost activity in their new home. They had been greeted by strange sounds, especially emanating from the attic.

"Definitely haunted," he assured us. Perhaps William Fenton's spirit isn't pleased with his not-so-perfect reputation in the eyes of Portland historians? Before we continued on to Lone Fir, the current owner told us to check out his Instagram, The Historic Fenton House, to follow along with the restoration process. How could we resist a photographic look inside? We both hit Follow instantly. Pictures include treasures like the mansion's original stained-glass door, as well as videos of peculiar finds, our favorite being the Victorian-era house "intercom," a crude sort of voice amplifier that we're just going to assume is haunted.

Finally, we made it to the main part of the walking tour. It's important to note that outside the cemetery was a collection of unhoused citizens in tents. This points to the disparity between places like the William D. Fenton House and spots where other Portlanders are living. Unfortunately, not so much has changed in two hundred years.

Sarah is passionate about representing the diversity of Portland in her tours. She explains, "Telling the stories of people whose histories have been overlooked by those who write the books has always been a passion for me, and part of our company's direction. In some ways, ghost tours are the easiest places to find stories of immigrant populations and women. However, telling the story in a way that doesn't sensationalize or romanticize victimization is a delicate balance. Looking for narratives outside the usual context of ghost stories has been one way that I have accessed stories of women and immigrants whose spirits have been wronged. And that's kind of at the heart of it; thinking from the perspective of who are the individuals doing the wrong, and whose soul most probably deserves torture, is a fascinating and worthwhile journey. Getting as much firsthand narratives and oral histories as possible is one way we explore these stories; going out of my way to learn about Chinese immigrants, for instance, or to think more deeply about people whose lives and deaths were footnotes to the stories of white men by doing more research, helps all of us understand the human story better."

As we entered the wrought iron gates of Lone Fir Cemetery, Sarah pointed first to an empty spot of land with no grave markers. It instead had a sign indicating the history of this seemingly unremarkable piece of the cemetery. What looked like an untouched lawn was actually the mass grave of many Portlanders, ones who had not been afforded the respect of their own resting place. In the late nineteenth and early twentieth centuries, she said, "more than 2,800 Chinese and Chinese American people were buried in Lone Fir Cemetery, and while many were exhumed and returned to China in accordance with their cultural practices, some of their bodies remain there." Sarah explained that many of them were railroad workers who had come to forge a better life in America, only to be greeted with racism and then ultimately buried in this mass grave, along with patients of nearby Hawthorne Asylum. It was a somber reminder that, just as in life, in death we're not treated equally. Thankfully, the city is rectifying this with a memorial that is being built in honor of these silent Portlanders. It is estimated to be finished in 2026.

As we crisscrossed through the foggy confines of the cemetery, Sarah shared tidbits about many of the gravestones. There were unique, carved wooden ones made to look like trees in honor of several craftsmen, as well as a decaying mausoleum for one of Portland's first craft beer makers. His last name was Bottler. No...we're not kidding. Quite a few other graves were properly gothic—mottled with moss or nearly unreadable from the cruel passage of time. Others were modern, adorned with smiling, laser-cut images of the deceased. It is clear that Portland and its surrounding area were steeped in dark history that resonated through the generations, exemplified by the "Keep Portland Weird" slogan. We don't want to spoil all the macabre stories Sarah told us, because we want you to make the gothic pilgrimage to the leaden gray skies of Oregon yourself. Go to AroundPortlandTours.com to book your tour with Sarah and Edwin.

The Shanghai Tunnel Tour

226 NORTHWEST DAVIS STREET

The last tour we took in Portland allowed us to explore the famed Shanghai Tunnels, which run underneath the city. According to *Travel Portland*, "Local lore has it that a labyrinth of interconnected basements, makeshift rooms, and low-ceilinged tunnels ran to the waterfront, making it easy to sneak illegal goods between shore and ship. Some say the tunnels were also used as secret passageways to underground  brothels, opium dens and gambling houses or as temporary prisons for kidnapped men and women." We heard tales of a ghost named Nina and sampled beers from the brewery upstairs, Old Town Pizza and Brewing. Our fun and knowledgeable guide brought us safely through numerous dark passages and regaled us with stories from history and legend. It was certainly a night we'll never forget.

The Benson Hotel Stairway Museum

309 SOUTHWEST BROADWAY

If you have the time to explore the Benson, whether you're staying there or not, we recommend checking out the unique stairwell museum. At nearly every floor there is a themed photography display focusing on everything from the history of Portland to the hotel itself, and even black-and-white photos of the famous Rose Parade the city is known for. Beware—we recommend taking an elevator to the top and working your way down. We learned from experience to climb DOWN the stairs instead of UP! Once we were at the top of the stairwell, sweating and out of breath, we realized the opposite direction would've been wiser...oops.

Even so, we enjoyed this free and physically active glimpse into a historic hotel. And we're very glad Benson's ghost wasn't waiting on the fourteenth floor (more on him later).

 The Pacific Northwest is full of tales of cryptids, including one passed down by lumberjacks called the Gumberoo. This creature, said to be shaped like a football meets hairless bear, has black skin that is bulletproof. These meat eaters, when not hibernating, are seeking food, so beware.

Movie Madness

4320 SOUTHEAST BELMONT STREET

Movie Madness is a must-see for movie fans. The rental store features over eighty thousand titles on DVD, Blu-Ray, and VHS in every genre imaginable. Grab a beer and a snack to wander the endless aisles of movies and authentic film props, or attend a movie showing in their miniplex. This nonprofit is open seven days a week and will bring back the nostalgia of going to your local video store to pick out movies for the weekend.

The Freakybuttrue Peculiarium

2234 NORTHWEST THURMAN STREET

It would be a downright shame if you visited Portland without going to the Freakybuttrue Peculiarium housed in two buildings on Thurman Street. Boasting an unforgettable spontaneous human combustion display, insect-stuffed candy, and our favorite dollhouse (think Sam Raimi gore meets David Cronenberg weirdness), the Peculiarium ($7 on Tuesdays) is way worth it. We giggled our way through the eccentric museum, taking SO many photos. These included constructed photo ops, like a mind-bending setup that is made to look like we're hanging from the side of a building, as well as posing as the subject of an alien autopsy.

Witch Paddle

WILLAMETTE RIVER

It makes sense that Portland has been called "the best place in the country to be a witch," as there is an annual Witch Paddle, in which hundreds of people dress up in their best witchy attire as they stand-up paddleboard on the Willamette River. This event, encouraged for those who have paddleboard experience, occurs around Halloween. Check the group's Facebook page for updates and plan your trip accordingly.

 Portland is home to a Mystic District, which features three unique shops in one block. The stores are Seagrape Soap, Brown Bear Herbs, and Magic Goes Mainstream.

WHERE TO SHOP

Powell's City of Books, Bookstore

1005 WEST BURNSIDE STREET

Powell's City of Books is the world's largest independent bookstore. And since it was a few days before Christmas when we visited, Powell's was absolutely hopping. Self-admitted bookworms, we entered the enormous store, immediately enchanted by the seemingly endless rows of books in a labyrinthine journey through various rooms. Thankfully there is a desk where free maps are handed out to help first timers like us. We recommend you snag one yourself, to make finding the horror section oh so much easier. Speaking of horror, Meg had to buy a book before leaving Powell's (*obvi*), so she chose the horror-holiday anthology mash-up *Hark the Herald Angels Scream* (2018), edited by Christopher Golden, featuring contemporary horror authors such as Scott Smith and Josh Malerman. It was a lovely holiday addition to her book collection that she'll always treasure. She also made sure to get a magnet and sticker so that she could commemorate our time in Portland. If you're looking to visit Powell's downtown (the flagship store, which boasts over one million books), you should give yourself plenty of time for browsing. There is also a coffee shop inside, as well as charming bookish gifts and a rare-book room that has limited weekend hours. If you want to access the rare books, you must sign in downstairs to get a pass. We think it's totally worth it, as there's nothing more gothic than lounging in a quiet room with antiquarian books surrounding you.

WHERE TO STAY

The Benson

309 SOUTHWEST BROADWAY

Stepping inside the Benson was truly one of our favorite highlights from the trip. We're sure you've heard the often-used expression that someone felt as though they were "transported through time," but we can genuinely say this was the feeling as we beheld the magnificence of the Benson, which has been at the pinnacle of Portland's finery since 1913. The hotel's website boasts, "Built by the millionaire innovator Simon Benson, this fabled European-style hotel was built to put Portland on the international map. Featuring Italian marble floors, Austrian crystal chandeliers, and Circassian walnut wood from the imperial forests of Russia." When we were there in December, the already lavish lobby was decorated for the holiday season with dozens of potted poinsettias and a towering tree. The centerpiece, surrounded by fellow tourists, was a gingerbread creation less like the charming frosting-smeared houses we make at home and more like something you'd see on the Food Network. A fifty-year-long tradition, the gingerbread display has a new theme every year. In 2022, the theme that greeted us was "Multnomah Falls," a confectionery ode to the nearby waterfall, made with over twenty pounds of chocolate and over one hundred and fifty pounds of homemade gingerbread! It was a *Willy Wonka and the Chocolate Factory*–like spectacle! So, you might be asking, *Okay, Kelly and Meg, this sounds lovely and all, but where's the spooky stuff?*

We chose to spend our first night in Portland at The Benson because of its dubious honor as being one of the most haunted places in the city.

As you veer off from the glittery lobby, it's not hard to imagine ghouls lurking in the darkened stairs leading to the lower floor. In fact, the most famous dead resident of the Benson is Simon Benson himself. Story goes that he was a teetotaler, so devoted to vanquishing alcohol from Portlanders that he was the first to install water fountains in the city. These are still outside the hotel today, providing city water for those not interested in a pint. The legend of Benson's ghost is that he dislikes when hotel patrons drink spirits and will often swat the glass from their hands! Obviously, our first task was to test this theory at the Palm Court Restaurant and Bar, located in the luxurious lobby of the Benson. After stowing our luggage with the helpful staff, we settled in for a scrumptious brunch with mimosas. (We know...it's a tough gig.) Champagne flutes in hands, we hoped Mr. Benson might give us a little otherworldly push. There was a cold draft, but it was more likely air emanating from the hotel's front door rather than the apparition of the hotel's former owner. While we didn't have trouble drinking our mimosas at the Benson, we'd recommend being careful while sipping your drinks... We'd hate for Mr. Benson to knock a martini down the front of your newest goth tee.

McMenamins Edgefield

2126 SOUTHWEST HALSEY STREET, TROUTDALE

It was obvious from the moment we were left on the stairs of McMenamins Edgefield that the building had not begun its life as a luxury hotel like The Benson. Its bricked walls and utilitarian windows screamed, *Order! Institution! Hospital!* The luxe artifice of The Benson was nowhere to be seen in this sliver of the Northwest woods. Inside, the artistic charm of the building hugs you, making you forget that it was once both a poor farm and a nursing home. This naturally means a lot of people died there in not-so-happy circumstances. Which, you guessed it, leads to the inevitability that it's bursting with ghost sightings.

McMenamins is a truly unique place, with long hallways covered in eclectic murals and framed photos. Sometimes our eyes didn't know where to look! There are no TVs in the rooms, but with plenty to enjoy, including a winery and brewery on property, as well as live music, you won't be hanging around in your room much anyway.

It's a casual place, where guests roam in the provided white robes to the popular soaking pool. In better weather, we were encouraged to walk the lush seventy-four-acre property with wineglass in hand, enjoying the many outbuildings restored from their former poor-farm days. We could imagine a lover of the macabre reveling in the hypnotic nature of Oregon, finding a hidden bench or crumbling fountain on which to read Shirley Jackson.

It was already pitch-black by the time we got there, so we busied ourselves in the restaurant and impressive gift shop. McMenamins, it seems, owns half of Portland, and the company is known to restore old buildings with questionable pasts for modern fun. This hotel leans into its history, pointing out the original use of rooms and selling books about ghost encounters.

It was built in 1911 with the original purpose of being a poor farm. This was essentially a workplace for people who were in desperate need of money, often unhoused or owing money to someone more powerful than themselves. At its height, the poor farm that later became McMenamins Edgefield was home to six hundred people. While a home for those experiencing poverty may sound rather nice, poor farms were notorious for overworking and punishing those who lived there. Anne Sullivan, known as Helen Keller's "miracle worker," spent her childhood in a poor farm (not this one in Portland) and testified to its horrid nature: "Residents at the Massachusetts poorhouse milled about like forgotten animals. As Anne and her brother slept on the institution's iron cots in a gigantic dormitory, rats ran up and down the spaces between beds." As we thought about what people went through within those walls, we had a sobering night's sleep.

While Meg somehow fell asleep, Kelly stayed awake to watch a show on her phone before going to bed. About 11:30 p.m., she decided it was time to turn off her device and get some much-needed sleep. As she removed her earbuds and set the phone on the nightstand, she noticed the figure of a man bent over next to her looking through Meg's suitcase! It appeared that he was wearing a tattered flannel shirt, and Kelly was TERRIFIED. She made eye contact, and she immediately sat up to alert Meg there was a man in our room. Just as she turned, he moved toward the opposite side of the room, away from the door, and disappeared.

Kelly's initial terror of thinking a man was in our room turned to fascination as she realized she may have just experienced her first ghost sighting! Needless to say, she didn't sleep much, or very well, for the remainder of the night. She didn't tell Meg what she witnessed until Meg woke up in the morning, and she made Kelly promise to wake her up next time she experiences anything spooky. Stay tuned.

WHERE TO EAT

Raven's Manor

235 SOUTHWEST FIRST AVENUE

If you're a goth who likes to plan ahead, make sure to reserve your spot at Raven's Manor long before you set your black boots in Portland. This new horror-themed bar is crazy popular, with limited seating. We tried to sneak in with no reservation, but after a long wait in line on the street (during which a murder of crows cawed at us in the twilight), we missed out on cocktails with names like Black Widow, Lilith, and Draught of Asphyxiation. *SIGH*. At least we got to peek at the sumptuous skull and raven decor before we were told there were no crushed-velvet seats for us. Next time we come to Portland, we're planning way ahead so we can get our hands on The Grilled Cheese of Darkness.

Old Town Brewing

5201 NORTHEAST MARTIN LUTHER KING JR. BLVD

Before or after your tour of the Shanghai Tunnels, stop by the Northeast location of Old Town Brewing for a slice of pizza, salad, and a beer. Old Town opened in 1974 in one of the oldest buildings in Portland, originally the Merchant Hotel. The restaurant is located inside the hotel lobby, and the window where you place your order is the original reception desk. Owner Adam Milne is a longtime fan of the restaurant, having fallen in love with the place when he was nine years old. He wants Old Town to be part of the revitalization of the downtown area. He said, "I wanted to come out of the pandemic and really be a part of the solution to making Portland better... So we started with that. How can we be a positive voice for Portland?" Part of the solution included extending their lease in the location for twelve years, offering haunted tunnel tours, and changing their beer can labels to reflect Portland's story with art and slogans celebrating the city. We enjoyed sampling several of their flagship beers and some specialty brews with fellow ghost tour participants. Cheers!

Voodoo Doughnut

22 SOUTHWEST THIRD AVENUE

For a sweet treat, head to Voodoo Doughnut. They were founded in 2003, right in Portland, and now have locations across the United States. According to their website, "Voodoo Doughnut created the gourmet doughnut category. Famous for introducing the world to the Bacon Maple Bar, Memphis Mafia, and The Cannolo, Voodoo Doughnut now offers more than fifty artisan flavor options, including twenty-five vegan options, with a focus on the guest experience, employee incentives, and giving back to the community through its charitable initiatives." We shared a classic voodoo-doll-shaped doughnut, and it was delicious. We recommend taking a taxi or rideshare to this location in downtown Portland.

A WOMAN YOU SHOULD KNOW

Charity Lamb
(1818–1879)

On our tour of Lone Fir Cemetery, we lingered in the Portland fog, December chill nipping at our cheeks as we took in the mass burial site. Our tour guide, Sarah, elaborated on the history of Hawthorne Asylum, ending on the story of one of its most well-known patients, Charity Lamb. The name sounded familiar...but maybe just because Charity Lamb sounds like a TikTok-famous sheep we'd probably follow. Turns out she was a real person with a past straight out of a horror movie.

Sarah, who has done extensive research on Lamb's life, told us the harrowing story of Charity, the first woman to be convicted of murder in Oregon. Charity had been married to an extremely abusive man, Nathaniel, who others in the neighborhood had deemed as such. She was often covered in bruises, as it seems Nathaniel had no compulsion to hide his hideous acts. He was even known to beat her when she was pregnant.

Charity and Nathaniel had come to Clackamas, Oregon, by way of the Oregon Trail in the 1850s with their five children, attempting to make a home in an unknown land. In 1854, the tumultuous marriage became even more dangerous when Charity helped their nineteen-year-old daughter with a love letter to a suitor of whom Nathaniel disapproved. For a week he screamed at Charity and even threatened death for this supposed transgression. Their children testified to this behavior later, pointing to an incident in which Nathaniel drew a shotgun on Charity. Scared for her life, Charity snapped, swinging an ax on her abusive husband at the dinner table, in front of the children! The wounds were severe, though it took a week for Nathaniel to succumb to his injuries. Charity was convicted of second-degree rather than first-degree murder, so she avoided the noose and was sent to a primitive prison in Oregon Territory until she was eventually remanded to the Hawthorne Asylum for the remainder of her life.

As someone who has been fascinated by the Lizzie Borden ax murder case since childhood, Meg was instantly intrigued by Charity Lamb. She had been seen being abused in front of her neighbors and family over the course of her marriage but still was torn away from her children forever and eventually buried in the mass grave beneath our feet. It was a poignant reminder of how harrowing life was in the pioneer days, especially for women. Another thing to caution: when we started to do online research into the case of Charity Lamb, there was quite a lot of misinformation. This included talk of motive revolving around a love affair. We're so glad we heard the story from an expert in Portland history who had done the proper research so we could tell you the real story. This is why reaching out to tour guides and local experts is so vital.

TRAVEL TIPS

1. Downtown Portland is quite walkable, but be aware of your safety. The area around Voodoo Doughnut was particularly questionable, and though it was heavily policed, we felt more comfortable taking a rideshare.

2. Book your guided tours for the beginning of your trip, so knowledgeable guides can suggest local treasures you can explore.

3. One of our favorite parts of traveling is talking to locals about their cities. There's no better opportunity to get to know someone than riding in their rideshare. A driver named William drove us to Troutdale and told us about his family history of vaudeville performing in Oregon. Don't be afraid to chat with people. You never know who you'll meet and what you'll learn.

4. Check out the iconic movie house from *The Goonies* (1985). It exists not far from Portland and was purchased by a fan in 2023. Owner Behman Zakeri intends to preserve the film's memory by redecorating the home to appear as it did in the movie, including a zip line! He told the *Washington Post*, "I'm just super excited to try to be the best I can be for the *Goonies* community."

5. For the weather in Portland, we recommend dressing in layers. The warm season lasts from June to September, so the other months may have wind, rain, and cold that will affect what you should plan to pack. And be sure to pack a raincoat for those rainy days.

OTHER SPOOKY PLACES AROUND THE STATE

Florence

The Heceta Lighthouse in Florence is considered one of the most haunted hotels in America. Now a bed-and-breakfast, the lighthouse was built in 1894 and is said to be haunted by a woman looking for her child.

Newport

One of our favorite horror movies of all time, *The Ring* (2002), filmed some of its scenes in Oregon. The Yaquina Head Lighthouse in Newport was featured as well as Oregon's Columbia River Gorge.

Eugene

A trip to Eugene, Oregon, will give you plenty of purported haunted places to visit, including the Shelton McMurphy Johnson House, a Victorian-era home that is now a museum; Art House, a former mortuary turned coffee shop and theater; and several cemeteries.

PROVIDENCE

RHODE ISLAND

POPULATION: 189,692

SPOOKIEST THING TO HAPPEN HERE

About twenty minutes outside of Providence in Exeter, Rhode Island, you may happen across the grave of Mercy Brown. The most famous interred resident of Chestnut Hill Cemetery, nineteen-year-old Brown lost her life in the winter of 1892. Mercy Brown's short life had been a tragic one; she'd had to endure watching both her beloved mother and sister die from tuberculosis before succumbing to the same condition.

Because of modern science, we know that the Brown family died from a highly contagious disease, but rural Rhode Islanders living on the cusp of the twentieth century had trouble understanding the Browns' misfortune. This, coupled with a mysterious dream and rampant gossip of deceased Mercy Brown stalking her loved ones like a vampire, led to a macabre decision made by the townspeople of Exeter.

Mercy's father, George Brown, allowed the exhumation of his daughters and wife in order to stop their vampiric designs on his dying son, Edwin. George believed that his dead family was feasting on the blood of Edwin, draining him slowly every night until he died. When Mercy's sister and mother were dug up by the townsfolk, they were obviously decomposed. But, when Mercy was exhumed, she was found to be oddly preserved. (She'd been dead only two months in the coldest time of year.) This unsettling image fanned the flames of those who believed she was a vampire. They removed Mercy's heart in order to make certain she left Edwin alone. Oh...and Edwin ate a bit of her heart in some ill-conceived notion to keep him alive. As you might've guessed, it didn't work, and Edwin, too, succumbed to tuberculosis. Mercy Brown's story, and ones similar in the area, briefly made Rhode Island the "Vampire Capital of America." Check out the episode "They Made a Tonic" from the TV series *Lore* (2017–2018) to learn more.

HIDDEN GEM WE DISCOVERED

The Arcade Providence

65 WEYBOSSET STREET

While on a walking tour of the city of Providence, we were led through the historic arcade. Built in 1828, it's the first enclosed shopping mall in the United States and an example of Greek Revival architecture. While it's absolutely stunning, what caught our eye inside the arcade was *NecronomiCon* Providence, a bookstore and shop that houses Lovecraft Arts and Sciences.

According to their website, they serve as "a networking center for scholars, authors, artists, and fans of the Weird literary world, inspired in part by Providence author H. P. Lovecraft and expanded upon by so many others. We strive to foster a vibrant and diverse global weird fiction and art community, and to provide a home for this community here in Providence."

They organize multiple events, including the biennial NecronomiCon Providence convention, talks, discussions, and workshops. We looked around at the unique collection of books and were thrilled to see a copy of our book *The Science of Women in Horror* (2020) on one of the shelves. From children's books to academic fare, this bookstore is a must-see for all horror fans.

MOST FAMOUS TRUE CRIME

Providence is known for its storied history of organized crime, full of imposing mob bosses. In 1975, eight thieves broke into a secret bank housed in the Hudson Fur Storage Company. They "looted as much as $34 million in cash, gems, jewelry, silver bars, and gold coins" belonging to well-known mafia boss Raymond L. S. Patriarca. It's believed these thieves were under the direction of mobster John Ouimette, who, despite spending the rest of his life in prison for the robbery plot, continued to run an impressive crime outfit until his death in 2017.

 # SPOOKY MOVIES AND BOOKS SET HERE

BOOKS

The Drowning Girl (2012) by
　　Caitlin R. Kiernan
Providence (2018) by
　　Caroline Kepnes
The Pallbearer's Club (2022) by
　　Paul Tremblay

MOVIES

The Witches of Eastwick (1987)
The Conjuring (2013)
Amityville: Evil Never Dies (2017)

WHAT TO DO

Providence Ghosts: Phantoms and Poltergeists Tour

VARIOUS MEETING SITES

US Ghost Adventures has dozens of tours all over the country, and they even are the current owners of the Lizzie Borden House. We've taken several tours with them and have been impressed with the knowledge and friendliness of the guides. Emily in Providence met us at night for the Phantoms and Poltergeists Tour, starting in Memorial Park. She held a glimmering old-fashioned lantern, which really set the ghostly mood. The first thing to note in the park was a sculpture known as the gun totem, a cement post affixed with different guns.

Things only got darker from there as Emily brought us on a chilly walk through the oldest part of Providence. Because of the old age of the buildings, nearly every one of them had a fascinating history. The Dexter House, for example, owned by Brown College, was once a coroner's establishment and now houses college students. She also told us of the John Brown House, where the legendary Roger Williams tree root is purportedly kept in the basement. But the Providence founder's final resting place came with a twisted tale.

In 1860 (nearly two hundred years after he died), the people of Rhode Island wanted to give Williams a properly ornate burial place, so they tracked down his remains in what was a backyard. They were shocked to discover that his body was missing! In its place was a tree root, along with some teeth and hair. His corpse had been essentially "eaten" by the root, which was eerily shaped like a man with legs. The bits of teeth and bone fragments were buried on the vista, and the root is still in the John Brown House, but it isn't officially on display anymore, and the staff at the John Brown House aren't always so keen to show it. Maybe it's haunted? Cursed? Looking for more bodies to feast on? If you get your eyes on it, let us know.

Fleur-De-Lys Studios

7 THOMAS STREET

As you walk up College Hill toward Brown University, a unique house steals your attention. There are many beautiful historic homes and churches to see, yet this one is something to behold. The Fleur-De-Lys Studios is a bright golden ocher, outlined in midnight blue. Commissioned by Sydney Richmond Burleigh in 1885, the house is considered Norman style, inspired by seventeenth-century European architecture. Grecian goddesses are painted on the stucco, giving the house a splendidly feminine aura. It was no surprise to us that the house is owned by the Providence Art Club, as it is truly an aesthetic marvel.

On our tour with Emily, we learned of a woman who had an art studio in the Fleur-De-Lys in the 1920s. She took her life with gas in the house and is known to haunt artists today in, naturally, creative ways, like leaving footprints in paint and messing with brushes. Meg was skeptical about this story of the woman at first, as Emily didn't mention her name, but after some research, she was able to find the actual newspaper clipping from the 1921 *New York Herald* telling of Angela O'Leary's death. A former student of the Rhode Island School of Design, locally known as "Ris-Dee," O'Leary was a talented and noted watercolorist of landscapes.

The article mentioned that her "fear of cancer" led to her suicide, with no further details.

While there are no original artworks available to view in Providence, we recommend you do an online search of Angela O'Leary's paintings. She had a colorful, vivid style that makes her death all the more poignant.

Another reason to check out the Fleur-De-Lys Studios is that it's featured in perhaps H. P. Lovecraft's most famous short story, "Call of the Cthulhu" (1926). A native of Providence, horror and science-fiction author H. P. Lovecraft is a hometown hero. There are remembrances of him everywhere, from painted mythical sea creatures adorning city walkways to Lovecraft Square at the intersection of Angell and Prospect. For those with a special place in their hearts for Lovecraft's brand of horror, they can take an official H. P. Lovecraft tour, which makes stops at the Fleur-De-Lys as well as Lovecraft's gravestone. On it is a special line written by Lovecraft in one of his letters and added to his grave forty years after his death by the city. It reads, *"I am Providence."*

As Lovecraft is an institution of the city, the Fleur-De-Lys is a local marvel. Just standing outside of the Fleur-De-Lys is worth the walk, but if you have a hankering to get inside, we recommend you search art exhibit events held by the Providence Art Club.

The Shunned House

Like the Fleur-De-Lys, the Shunned House has remained in its spot on Benefit Street for hundreds of years, a reliable building in the midst of change. The house, as modest as the Fleur-De-Lys is ornate, was built in the 1760s and was well known to H. P. Lovecraft, as his aunt Lillian lived there. He would visit her and often stay the night. The house got its dubious name from Lovecraft's fictional novella *The Shunned House* (1937), in which everyone who is unfortunate to live inside becomes violently ill or dies.

As we stood outside the rather inconspicuous house, Emily mentioned that long before Aunt Lillian lived there, it was believed that a French werewolf had been in residence. Yes...you read that right: *a French werewolf*. Rumor was that a French murderer (who blamed his deeds on his werewolf alter ego) fled his country and came to the shores of Rhode Island, inhabiting the Shunned House. Our research didn't uncover an actual culprit, as the most famous French killers to blame the wolf within, Gilles Garnier and Peter Stubbe, existed two hundred years before the Shunned House was built. (If you haven't read about these two fascinating cases, we strongly encourage you to do a Google search and creep yourself out.)

Lovecraft was inspired by the rumors; therefore, in his novella the sickness is caused by such a werewolf, with a dash of vampiric tendencies, feeding on the residents' life force. It's easy to draw similarities between this fictional horror story and the true Mercy Brown incident. Lingering outside the Shunned House reminded us of how murky the line is between make-believe and authentic monsters.

The Providence Athenaeum

251 BENEFIT STREET

A Greek Revival built in 1836, the Providence Athenaeum is a horror fan's dream. Its pillars and wrought iron lampposts are the aesthetic epitome of gothic. Created before the advent of public libraries, the Athenaeum has been at the heart of Providence's literary scene since long before H. P. Lovecraft spun his monstrous tales. It is a member's library, meaning locals can pay a fee in order to have lending privileges. Visitors like us are encouraged to pay a $5 donation when we enter. As nonmembers we have to relegate our reading and research to inside the building.

It was obvious from the moment we entered the Athenaeum that this was going to be our new favorite place. The book nerd in Meg (which, let's be real, is always hovering at the surface) fully bloomed at the sight of an endless supply of antique tomes. Flanked by marble statues, these rows of books have been privy to literary history. The card catalog even has a marked reference card of a book Edgar Allan Poe checked out. Other famous visitors to the Athenaeum include poet Walt Whitman and writer Charlotte Perkins Gilman, whose "The Yellow Wallpaper" (1892) is a must-read for any goth. When Meg read it freshman year in college, she knew devoting her life to female-driven horror was her life's calling... so, not to use hyperbole, but Gilman's story changed Meg's life. Knowing that the author had passed through that very door and breathed in the same book dust was darkly magical.

We can't recommend a visit to the Providence Athenaeum enough. After a view of an original oil portrait of Poe next to his Providence love (more on her later), check out the lower level, where you can ogle first printings of such classics as Whitman's *Leaves of Grass* (1855) and Louisa May Alcott's *Little Women* (1868). Oh, and hit the gift shop on your way out if dark academia is your chosen goth aesthetic.

And as you're making your way back onto Benefit Street, it's bad luck not to drink from the Gothic Revival marble fountain in front of the Athenaeum. Donated in 1873 by neighbor Anna Eddy Richmond, the stunning drinking fountain is inscribed with "Come Hither Every One That Thirsteth," and rumor is that "all those who drink from it are bound to always return to Providence."

When we passed the fountain on our night tour with Emily, she mentioned that Poe's ghost has been known to linger around the fountain. He even liked to follow those who drank the water, haunting them in their homes.

Unfortunately, when we tried to drink from the legendary fountain, it was turned off for the winter. But we did each wiggle a finger in the melted snow inside. The pale visage of Edgar Allan Poe has not shown up in the shadows of our houses yet. But we hope the legend of Richmond Fountain is true and that we'll be back in Providence (in the summer so we can drink that ghost water!).

Finally, as our tour was winding down, Emily asked if either of us had ever seen a ghost. Kelly told her the story of what I saw when we visited Portland, Oregon. As she finished the story, Emily said she had goose bumps. Just then, a man who had not heard Kelly tell the story walked past us and said a single word: "Resentful." We all looked at each other, but the man kept walking. "Well, that's never happened before," Emily chuckled. But the scary thing was, he looked just like the ghost Kelly had seen that night in Portland. Had he followed us here? Was it a coincidence? We will report back with any updates.

We also got eerie feelings as we ended the tour at Brown University, where we heard stories of ghosts who still haunt the gates and buildings on the premises. University Hall, once used as a barracks and hospital for American troops during the Revolutionary War, has many tall, looming windows where people have seen soldiers peering out. We were thankful to be heading back to our nice, cozy hotel room where we hadn't yet heard the ghost stories for the premises.

An Overnight Trip to Fall River, Massachusetts

We're including this trip to Massachusetts because Providence is just a twenty-minute drive (or a forty-minute bus ride) from the notorious town. Fall River is home to the Lizzie Borden House, and to say Meg was excited to finally visit Fall River is quite an understatement. She's been fixated on Lizzie Borden since she'd discovered her in the film *The Legend of Lizzie Borden* (1975), starring Elizabeth Montgomery.

If you don't know what happened, here's an abridged version.

In August of 1892, husband-and-wife duo Andrew and Abby were brutally murdered with an ax in their home in the middle of the day. The only viable suspect was Andrew's thirty-two-year-old daughter, Lizzie. She was put on trial for the double murder and eventually deemed innocent by a jury of twelve men. Despite this, the denizens of Fall River and the world beyond still believe Lizzie is the murderer.

Fall River became a magically gothic locale in Meg's mind, especially after she read an account of the Borden murders by a Fall River resident, Victoria Lincoln, called *A Private Disgrace: Lizzie Borden by Daylight* (1967). Visiting Fall River has been at the top of Meg's proverbial bucket list, and here we were. In January. In the freezing sleet. But even that couldn't wipe the grins from our faces. We fought our way up the steep, slippery sidewalk to Lizzie Borden's former home, which now offers tours and overnight accommodations. It sits in an innocuous neighborhood, next to an apartment building and across from an equally historic Catholic church that Borden housekeeper Bridget Sullivan attended.

We'll never forget punching in the code on the front door (which we got from booking a room for the night) and stepping into the house where two of the most notorious murders in America occurred. It was especially surreal because the house is kept in the style of the turn of the twentieth century. The moldings and floors are original, and every room is full of authentic Borden family belongings. These include books, baubles, and family photographs. Our favorite touch was the Christmas tree, adorned with bloody axes and pears (a hint to Lizzie's paper-thin alibi). There were other cheeky items to spot, like a Lizzie Borden bobblehead and the sheet music for "You Can't Chop Your Poppa Up in Massachusetts" waiting on the music stand of a piano. If only we knew how to play it. Oh, there was also a costume from the Elizabeth Montgomery film, so it was a full-circle moment for a lifelong goth girl.

While all of this is fun, we couldn't help but feel the sense that bad things had happened there. This was especially vivid in the room where Andrew Borden was killed. A replica of the settee was placed where it had been in 1892. There is even a cutout of Andrew's face to show the position of how he was found.

This room, as well as another sitting room and the dining room, all downstairs, are considered the common area, which the overnight guests are allowed to use. Sitting right where Andrew Borden had been axed was sobering, a visceral reminder that real people were involved.

After some socializing downstairs, we made our way up the narrow staircase. All the while Meg was thinking, *This is where Lizzie was standing when the police came... This is where Abby's body was visible in the guest room. This is where...*

Buzzing with this intimate proximity to history, we were awed by our room for the night. We'd chosen the Lizzie and Emma Suite, surprised to find it was two rooms in one. Like the public rooms, this one, separated into two sleeping areas, was adorned with Borden-era furniture and decorations. Kelly was kind enough to let Meg sleep in Lizzie's room, while she took the smaller section that had belonged to Emma, Lizzie's older sister.

We participated in two events at the Lizzie Borden House. Like several of the ghost tours we went on, these were put on by US Ghost Adventures. We did the two-hour ghost hunt that night. Despite the icky weather, the ghost hunt was packed. We listened to a brief history of the murders, as well as the tragic case of Lizzie Borden's great-aunt Eliza Darling Borden, who killed her children by throwing them in a well. She then slit her own throat, in what we can assume in retrospect was an act of postpartum psychosis. Eliza is purported to haunt the Bordens' cellar, as her own nearby home is gone.

After a rundown of ghost-hunting equipment, we were separated into two groups. Our first stop was the cellar. Meg placed a motion-activated music box in the corner known as "Eliza's spot." Others used dowsing rods, heat cameras, and ghost communication apps on their phones that we hadn't known existed until that moment. As ghost-hunting novices, we were probably a bit impatient, being more observant than active. Meg was more interested in the history of the cellar, imagining where they found the bloody bucket Lizzie had said was for her menstrual rags but could've been hiding murder evidence. No ghosts popped up in the cellar, or upstairs during the rest of the tour. Even so, we had fun learning about electromagnetic field meters, known as EMF readers, while watching more experienced ghostbusters.

For Meg, the absolute highlight of the tour was the hour-long historical house tour the next day. Our tour guide was extremely knowl-edgeable. Meg's loath to admit he might've even known *a little bit* more than her on the subject of the Borden murders. Maybe. He brought us from room to room, showing us more than we were able to see as night guests. On the second floor we saw the room where Abby, Lizzie's step-mother, lost her life, and the third floor attic, originally the small quar-ters of Bridget, had been expanded for more guest rooms.

Second to the historic tour, our favorite place was the gift shop, located in a separate building behind the house. It is stuffed with Borden T-shirts, teddy bears, key chains, ornaments, books, and SO much more. You can probably imagine the damage we did in there...not with an ax. If you're like Meg and buy a rubber ax splashed with fake blood at Lizzie Borden's house, we recommend you ship it home. Or you might be stopped at airport security like she was, where four stern TSA agents handled the ax and chewed her out for bringing it on the plane.

The Biltmore/Graduate

11 DORRANCE STREET

When we were researching where to stay in Providence, there was one clear choice: the Graduate Hotel. Built in 1922, the hotel was originally called the Biltmore and was the only luxury hotel in the city at the time. Numerous famous people stayed at the hotel, as well as some criminal ones (as we learned previously from our tour of the city), and it is considered one of the most haunted hotels in the United States. Guests have claimed to hear laughter and locks turning and to see apparitions. While we were able to sleep comfortably at the Graduate, we can understand the possibility of spotting ghosts on the premises. The architecture, historic furniture, and vintage items on display gave us a feeling of traveling back in time. We appreciated the multiple bars and restaurants on site as well as a lovely coffee shop to grab breakfast in the mornings. Another convenient aspect of the hotel was its proximity to the walking tours we booked. One even began in the lobby of the hotel.

WHERE TO EAT

Justine's

11 OLNEYVILLE SQUARE

This delightful speakeasy was a short ride from our hotel, and how to enter was a mystery. With no sign visible above the door, we read ahead of time to look for lingerie in the window display. We spotted some and entered carefully. A bouncer greeted us and led us past a curtain to a lovely 1920s-style bar. We enjoyed a cocktail called the Mary Pickford, with rum, maraschino liqueur, pineapple juice, and grenadine, and a glass of champagne. The atmosphere was welcoming and fun, and the drinks were reasonably priced. We will be back.

Hide

55 CROMWELL STREET

Our next stop was another speakeasy in Providence called Hide, located under the George restaurant in downtown Providence. We happened to arrive just as a comedy show was starting, so we bellied up to the bar and settled in for a night of entertainment. The speakeasy serves small plates and desserts, and features other forms of entertainment, such as live music.

Union Station Brewery

36 EXCHANGE TERRACE

After a walking tour of Providence, we stopped for lunch at Union Station Brewery and had some of the best tacos of our lives. Opened in 1993 and considered Rhode Island's first brewpub, the brewery prides itself in serving rotating beers and classic American tavern food in a charming and beautiful neighborhood.

Massimo Ristorante

134 ATWELLS AVENUE

Although it was perhaps not the most obvious choice for brunch, we chose to go to Massimo based on its reviews and reputation. We were so glad we did. First, we were served a "mimosa bar" with a choice of juices, and then we could order either breakfast or lunch food for our entrées. We chose lunch and had the most decadent ricotta ravioli and bread. Local recommendations have never led us astray when we travel, so we encourage you to ask others what you should try while you're in their town.

And don't forget to have a "coffee milk" before your Providence vacation is over. History tour guide James told us it's the official state drink (we didn't know that was a thing), and Meg made sure to have one at the airport on our way to our next vacation. Served on ice, it's basically like chocolate milk, but the syrup is coffee flavored instead. Definitely a New England treat!

A WOMAN YOU SHOULD KNOW

Sarah Helen Whitman
(1803–1878)

Before we stepped on Providence soil, neither of us had heard of this absolute gothic queen. Whitman (no relation to Walt) lived down Benefit Street from the Athenaeum, and as a lifelong writer and reader, she spent much of her free time there. She was a staple of the rich artistic and literary scene of Providence, as evidenced by her presence there even today. Her spirit, both literally and metaphorically, is believed to inhabit the Athenaeum. She championed local authors and curated others to do talks and readings in Providence.

It was obvious from the several tours we took that Whitman was best known because she was briefly the fiancée of Edgar Allan Poe. They, indeed, fell in love in Providence, no doubt because of their mutual love of poetry and fiction. The more macabre and brooding the better.

While their friendship endured, their love story did not. Whitman didn't want her betrothed to drink alcohol, so when an anonymous note was sent to her at the Athenaeum, saying that Poe had been seen drinking at a bar two days before their wedding (you can sit in the exact spot where Whitman was when the note was delivered, and yes, we definitely did), she was livid. Apparently, when Whitman received news of Poe's carousing, she ran from the Athenaeum the few blocks to her house, where, in a state of grief, she swiftly knocked herself out with a handkerchief of chloroform. It's just like something straight out of a Poe short story! When she awoke on a fainting couch, Poe was kneeling beside her, begging for her forgiveness. But like a true, formidable gothic girl, Whitman held strong and ended their engagement. Poe died ten months later, many think from alcohol poisoning, though the speculation continues.

While this story of Sarah Whitman was intriguing, it was really when we did research on her after our trip that she truly became endeared to us as a feminist force. Thanks to the book *Break Every Bond: Sarah Helen Whitman in Providence: Literary Essays and Selected Poems* (2019) by Brett Rutherford, we were able to learn about her life before and after Poe.

She was a huge proponent of his work, as well as that of Coleridge, Shelley, and Goethe. Her literary essays compiled in Rutherford's book are impressive, and we were especially moved by her writing in response to people who had put Poe in a bad light after his death. She was a fierce defender, despite his inability to remain truthful in their courtship. Whitman was also a talented poet in her own right and, as far as we're concerned, the true crown jewel of Providence.

 What does the only court case in American history to use spectral evidence to convict a killer have to do with a restaurant? Quite a bit. In 1673 in Portsmouth, Rhode Island, seventy-three-year-old Rebecca Cornell was found dead on her bedroom floor, lying half in her fireplace. Her death was presumed to be an accident. Her ghost appeared to her brother asking to look at her body again. He told the police, who discovered a stomach wound, which implicated her son in the murder. The Valley Inn Restaurant now resides in the same spot as the murder and is said to be haunted.

⏩ We were impressed to discover so many female-owned breweries in Rhode Island, including Narragansett and Crooked Current Brewing Company. According to an article in *Edible Rhody,* "Humans have been brewing and consuming beer for well over seven thousand years. For most of that time, the keepers of that time-honored tradition were women. In Europe during the late Middle Ages, female brewers wore tall pointed hats in order to be more visible in crowded marketplaces. They used cauldrons for brewing and retained cats to keep grain-eating mice at bay. To signal that beer was available to sell, they would hang a broom outside of their stalls. When the Reformation period arrived in the 1500s, these women were framed as witches by Protestant and Catholic churches vying to gain more followers. Despite being thus vilified, women didn't stop working as brewers."

TRAVEL TIPS

1. Like many other New England cities, Providence is very old. This means many of the sidewalks are in disrepair—great for spooky ambience, not so great for those who have accessibility concerns. Plan ahead and contact tour operators to get a rundown on sidewalk conditions and accessibility.

2. In a mood for a horrifying day trip? The Conjuring House, located in Burrillville, Rhode Island, about forty minutes from Providence, is where the Perron family lived in the 1970s. Their paranormal experiences inspired the first *The Conjuring* (2013). The colonial house, built in 1736, offers traditional tours as well as ghost investigations that you can participate in.

3. Want to learn even more about the Lizzie Borden case? Read *The Trial of Lizzie Borden* (2019) by Cara Robertson. You can also enjoy a more fictionalized take on the murders thanks to the film *Lizzie* (2018) and *Lizzie the Musical*, in which Borden and housekeeper Bridget Sullivan are lovers.

4. If you book a room at the Lizzie Borden House, know that you won't have access to your room at tour times. This means if you're staying more than one night, you'll have to pack up all your things and store them elsewhere. Read all the rules to make sure they work for you.

5. While we took a rideshare to Fall River, you can also take a forty-minute bus ride from Providence for as little as $2.

AUSTIN

TEXAS

POPULATION: 964,177

SPOOKIEST THING TO HAPPEN HERE

The Tragedies at Moore's Crossing

Near the Austin airport spans Moore's Crossing, an iron pedestrian bridge often used by hikers and bikers. During the day it looks like any bridge you might find across America. At night it's a different story. Because of its storied history, Moore's Crossing is known to be one of the most actively haunted places in the city.

When it was first built in 1884, citizens were so thrilled they held a parade in its honor. In 1921 a harrowing event, still considered the greatest rainstorm in the continental U.S., in a consecutive eighteen hours, killed six people in the Onion River below. Because of the floods, Moore's Crossing was raised higher in 1922. It is said that the ominous history continued, as a white man was hanged on the bridge by a mob because of his romantic relationship with a Black woman. Many witnesses have spoken of seeing the man hanging at night from his noose, or even hearing the creak and sway of his demise.

One anonymous blogger told of their own paranormal experience at Moore's Crossing in the 1980s, when cars were still allowed to cross.

"Just as we got in the middle of the bridge, my wife spotted a pedestrian standing to the right of the car, holding on to one of the support wires, waiting for us to cross the bridge. She was afraid I might hit him if he stepped out into our path. As we passed the man, my wife made a startled sound and asked me if I saw the man standing on the side of the bridge. She said he waved at her as we past [*sic*] him and that he was dressed strangely. I quickly looked up into the rearview mirror to see what she was talking about and saw no one. I stopped the car and rolled back the car to where she had seen the man standing. He wasn't there. I did recall seeing something out of the corner of my eye as we passed. An image of a young man standing there. My wife had a better look at him than I had. Just who was this person and how did he disappear so quickly without us seeing where he had gone?" Other witnesses have claimed to see people in early 1900s garb crossing the bridge, as even more have seen strange orbs of light, which are often associated with paranormal phenomenon. If you're brave enough to trek across Moore's Crossing at night, we encourage you to bring a bright flashlight.

HIDDEN GEM WE DISCOVERED

The Jackalope Bar

404 EAST SIXTH STREET

When's the first time you heard of the elusive jackalope? A menacing creature that's part bunny, part antelope, all violence. Okay, that might be pushing it. As for Meg, she'll always remember her first time learning about the jackalope in an episode of *America's Funniest Home Videos* (1989–). All the canned laughter was a clue that the horned beast was not actually real. A girl can dream.

The fictional jackalope is actually less fierce and way cuter than anything, including the taxidermic example at Austin's Museum of the Weird. It's believed that the American myth of the jackalope evolved from both sightings of infected rabbits as well as from a taxidermist. "The *New York Times* attributes the popularization of the jackalope to Douglas Herrick (1920–2003) of Douglas, Wyoming, who in 1932 created and sold the first taxidermy 'jackalope.' These taxidermy mounts became hugely popular, with many thousands being made and sold by Herrick's brother and son." Come to the Jackalope Bar (there are two locations in Austin) to "ride" the saddled jackalope. Stay for the award-winning burgers and cocktails with names like Salty Bitch.

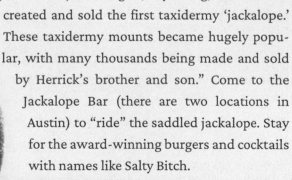

SPOOKY MOVIES AND BOOKS SET HERE

BOOKS

11/22/63 (2011) by Stephen King

A Cosmology of Monsters (2019) by Shaun Hamill

Hell Hath No Sorrow Like a Woman Haunted (2022) by R. J. Joseph

MOVIES

Frailty (2001)

Bubba Ho-Tep (2002)

X (2022)

 # MOST FAMOUS TRUE CRIME

Ax murders have a particular vintage sheen. They seem especially brutal in the heart of America, when families are struck down in such a violent manner. As true crime fans we've read *Man on the Train* (2017) by Bill James and Rachel McCarthy James, about a spate of ax murders that occurred across the country, from Iowa to New England, that were seemingly random and committed by a man who rode the extensive railroad on the cusp of the twentieth century. There is also the "New Orleans Axe Man," another unidentified murderer who favored the farm tool from 1918 to 1919. And we'd be remiss not to again bring up that mistress of the ax, Lizzie Borden, accused of killing her parents in 1892.

In 1884, Austin was unfortunately home to a similar madman. Known as the "Servant Girl Annihilator" (meh), "Austin Axe Murderer" (blah), and the "Midnight Assassin" (better), he stalked the shadows of Austin, killing and maiming both men and women with an ax, as well as with knives. He was known to leave something sharp sticking out from his victims' ears. Similar to Jack the Ripper, he would often drag his mutilated victims outside. And, yes, there was rumor, though it was never proven, that the Midnight Assassin and Jack the Ripper could be one and the same. Over a terrifying year in which Austinites feared for their safety, eight people lost their lives. These included children like teenager Eula Phillips and eleven-year-old Mary Ramey. The Midnight Assassin then disappeared into the Texan hills, leaving the city reeling. If you want to learn more about Austin's ax-wielding Midnight Assassin, we recommend esteemed true crime reporter Skip Hollingsworth's book *The Midnight Assassin: Panic, Scandal, and the Hunt for America's First Serial Killer* (2016).

 # WHAT TO DO

Museum of the Weird

412 EAST SIXTH STREET

Our first stop was Austin's well-known ode to the bizarre, Museum of the Weird. Just a short walk from the Driskill, the museum is housed among buildings marked with history plaques. Everywhere we turned there was something to discover, even before we made it inside. For thirteen bucks (our lucky number again) you can peruse several rooms of artifacts that we can attest are, indeed, weird. Our favorite aspect of this quirky museum is that it really is in the business of preserving the legacy of people like P. T. Barnum and others who created tourist attractions.

There is history to read around every corner, accompanied by fictional creatures that have long dazzled crowds, like the Fiji Mermaid and the aforementioned jackalope. While these things are not inherently real, Museum of the Weird sees the value in maintaining these exhibits for history's sake.

It would be impossible for us to list everything there is to look at. Some favorites were the wax figure room, which leaned into horror with actually pretty decent wax statues of Boris Karloff, Vincent Price, and others. There are also gross-out items like a six-year collection of toe and fingernail clippings. Just, why? We also enjoyed the real prop from *Gremlins 2: The New Batch* (1990), which showcased how the filmmakers moved those damn gremlins.

Museum of the Weird is a must-see in Austin, and a great way to hide away from the heat if you're cold-blooded like we are.

Alamo Drafthouse

14028 US-183 HIGHWAY

Austin is known for its vibrant art scene, as a rebellious piece of Texas that doesn't look or act like anywhere else in the state. Its world famous "Welcome to Austin" mural is an Instagram favorite, live music is thrumming its hypnotic beat every night downtown, and the SXSW Film Festival is a major event that takes over the city every spring.

It's no wonder Alamo Drafthouse has found success in a city with a penchant for creativity. Founded two decades ago in Austin by Tim and Karrie League, Alamo Drafthouse has now spread like a cinematic virus across the country. Only this is the kind of bug you want to catch! On their website they explain the philosophy of their one-of-a-kind movie-going experience: "We don't just want to be another multiplex. Everyone who works at Alamo Drafthouse, from the managers to the servers to the kitchen staff, is passionate about film. To us, an obscure foreign language drama can be just as worthy of attention and fanfare as the latest entry in the Marvel Cinematic Universe."

From the moment you walk into Alamo Drafthouse, you sense the difference. They *care* about movies. The one we visited, in Lakeline, was *Planet of the Apes* (1968) themed. Okay, maybe not our favorite movie, but they nailed the decor with statues, posters, and a deep red and orange color scheme that evoked Charlton Heston and those damn dirty apes. Just going to the lobbies of all the Alamo Drafthouses in town would be well worth it, as the Mueller cinema is a tribute to *Close Encounters of the Third Kind* (1977), while the others are themed after two of our favorite movies, *The Little Shop of Horrors* (1986) and *The Shining* (1980).

There are tons of fun events that happen at Alamo Drafthouse, like Terror Tuesday. Instead of showing only new releases, on Tuesday evenings they give horror fans the chance to experience films we may never have gotten the chance to see on the big screen. These vary from slashers like *Pieces* (1982) to more campy fare like *Gremlins 2: The New Batch* (1990). They also have movie "mockathons" where comedians lovingly riff on films in the spirit of *Mystery Science Theater 3000* (1988–1999). And we discovered they have something called "movie parties." We attended our very own movie party, and it didn't disappoint, especially because it was for Kelly's all-time favorite...*Evil Dead II* (1987). When we entered theater three, we were immediately greeted with three items that came with our movie ticket: a mini Necronomicon (cute), an edible eyeball (yum), and a soft chainsaw (groovy).

Before the film, they played old Sam Raimi/Bruce Campbell short films that were made before *Evil Dead* (1981). The energy was great—horror fans were happy—when the host of the movie party came running

on the stage dressed as Bruce Campbell's Ash Williams. He did a decently deadpan possessed-hand impression before starting off the party with the rules (we can quote during the movie, but no other talking; use the props at certain times for added fun, like eat the eyeball when the demon's eye lands in a mouth on-screen). He also brought volunteers up for a friendly *Evil Dead II* competition. Our favorite part was probably the unexpected confetti cannon that was set off at the climax, as well as the camaraderie of horror fans converging together on a Monday night to revel in what we truly love. When you're in Austin, plan ahead so you can attend your own movie party, or Terror Tuesday, or even Weird Wednesday. It's a film experience you won't soon forget. Oh, and if you're wondering, we saved our eyeballs for a rainy day.

Bat Watching on Congress Bridge

CONGRESS AVENUE

While we were in a hotel bar in Pittsburgh, we got to talking to a fellow Minnesotan. She lives in Austin in the winter, and so when we told her that was our next stop, she immediately yelled, "BATS!" Color us intrigued. Thankfully she elaborated, informing us about a huge colony of bats that live beneath the Congress Bridge. In 1980 a renovation of the bridge inadvertently created an ideal cave for migrating bats. Since then, the bat population has exploded. Instead of treating these goth pets like a nuisance, Austinites have embraced the flying animals, highlighting bat watching as a unique way to enjoy the city. Even in the airport there is bat photography, as well as subtle nods, like a Batini at the Driskill Bar. It's an Instagram-worthy cocktail with hibiscus that makes for a decadent vampiric purple.

The best time to watch the bats depart from their cozy home beneath Congress Bridge is about late March through early fall. These fuzzy nocturnal cuties fly out together at sunset, searching for food. Once the first bats leave, it can take up to forty-five minutes for all to follow. Since nature is tough to rely on, the bats can play coy. Unfortunately, they did not make an appearance for us. Despite this, there are tours built around seeing the bats, including a guided sunset kayak beneath the bridge. Meg thinks bats are adorable, but she has a fear of lots of flapping around her, so she's guessing the bats were just sensitive to her phobia. Gothic kings, queens, and everyone in between! If you, on the other hand, enjoy lots of flapping around you, we suggest you hit the bridge no later than seven thirty and plan on bringing snacks, because the bats may not make an appearance until as late as nine thirty. And if you're curious, they are Mexican free-tailed bats, a medium-size bat with wrinkled little faces that are known to fly quite fast. They love to eat moths and pretty much any insects. While they aren't the fearsome bloodsucking bats of Dracula's castle, they are an iconic piece of Austin's quirky landscape.

Zilker Botanical Garden

2220 BARTON SPRINGS ROAD

Goths appreciate nature, especially when it comes with a dash of whimsy. Zilker Botanical Garden is an expansive park open year-round with many alluring sections. These include a Japanese koi pond, a butterfly trail, and even a charming pioneer village. There's so much to see that we recommend you prepare for the Texas sun with a Lydia Deetz–style hat and a copious amount of sunscreen.

There are many events held at Zilker that if you're lucky enough to catch, you should brave the heat, like the Woodland Faerie Trail, which opens every Memorial Day for the summer. Locals can sign up for a plot on the trail where they make miniature homes for "fae folk." The only rule is that these houses must be constructed of natural materials. This leads to a magical trail of tiny moss, wooden, and stone structures where fae can find refuge, and that we can tour.

Another popular event is the Surreal Garden, which occurs every spring. A nightly soirée on weekends, the Surreal Garden is a neon-lit ode to the strange and unusual. Interactive art sculptures, surreal performers, and botanical neon art make for a lush experience.

The Texas Chainsaw Massacre Day Trip

1073 TX-304, BASTROP

We are huge fans of the original *The Texas Chainsaw Massacre* (1974)—its take on America's avoidance of the reality of meat production, its usage of true ghoul Ed Gein's skin masks, that chainsaw-wielding weirdo chasing down annoying teens. It has it all, and many believe *The Texas Chainsaw Massacre* was the bloody catalyst to the slasher boom that had its pinnacle in the 1980s. Austin-born filmmaker Tobe Hooper naturally picked his hometown to bring Leatherface to life. Thankfully for us, cinematic history has been preserved by locals so we can get in on the chainsaw fun.

In Bastrop, about forty minutes from downtown Austin, you can roll up to the gas station from the film. Inside is a horror-fan Mecca, stuffed to the rafters with horror merch, and *of course* serving nummy barbecue that we can't promise doesn't have Leatherface's latest victim ground in. But, hey, that's the fun. You'll know you're in the right place when you see the sign that says, "WE SLAUGHTER." If that's not enough proximity to the massacre, you can book a cabin (they have AC!) or a campsite on the gas station's property. Just don't blame us if you hear a chainsaw revving in the middle of the night. We warned you. Check out Texasgasstation.com to keep apprised of their events, too. They often have horror celebrities stop by for signings.

On the opposite side of Austin from Bastrop, about an hour from downtown, sits Hooper's in Kingsland. Hooper's was recently given its moniker in honor of the late Tobe Hooper for his contribution not only to the Austin film community but to the horror world at large. Hooper's restaurant is in the restored house that was used for Leatherface and his family in the 1974 film. Don't worry, they've swept out the chicken feathers and human bones. Now, it's a beautifully decorated brunch and dinner spot that doesn't forget to pay homage to the film. There are autographs from the filmmakers and actors on the wall, and cheeky cocktail names, like Grandpa Sawyer, that true fans will enjoy with a wink.

WHERE TO SHOP

The Glass Coffin: Vampire Parlor, Horror Shop

3009 NORTH INTERSTATE HIGHWAY 35

There are some places that feel as if they exist to take our money. The Glass Coffin is definitely on the top of that list, because we wanted literally *everything*. A former home tucked underneath an underpass of I–35, the Glass Coffin could fool any unsuspecting passerby. If you pass too quickly, the shop could just be the house of a Halloween aficionado— you know the type, because you probably are one. The kind who keeps their Halloween decorations up all year. In the front yard, a werewolf and skeleton watch the traffic, waiting for horror fans to stop by and shop. Thankfully we'd done our research. We knew this was no house but a store bursting with the sorts of merch we'd sell our souls for.

Each room in the house has been converted to feel just as it promises, like the dark Victorian vampire parlor of our dreams. Spooky music serenaded us as we filled our black baskets. Meg bought an Edgar Allan Poe coloring book, crystals for her growing collection of witchy goods, and handmade soap with the scent of a forest night. Not that she'd be goth enough to actually spend a night in the forest. That's for horror-movie victims. She'll just sniff her soap, thanks.

The Glass Coffin's goods lean heavily into the aesthetic of vintage horror. They concentrate more on the spiderwebbed environs of Dr. Frankenstein's lab rather than the bright neon of a modern horror fan's postered walls. Step aside, modern slashers—Edgar Allan Poe is the rock star here. There is plenty of witch paraphernalia, including jars full of spell ingredients and freshly wrapped sage bundles. As newbie tarot and oracle card collectors, we were pleased to go through their collection. We almost bought the Guillermo del Toro tarot set. But our baskets were starting to feel heavy.

The Glass Coffin is an absolute must-visit if you're in Austin. Even if you don't have money to spend, the ambience is worth stepping through the front door. They also hold a number of events. To say we almost cried over our missing the upcoming "Easterween" celebration is not an understatement. They advertise photos with Bunnicula, an appearance by the Sanderson Sisters of *Hocus Pocus* (1993), goth vendors, tarot readings, and a "goth Easter egg hunt." You read that right, reader—an actual egg hunt for people like us. We wouldn't have minded plotting a way to stay longer in Austin for the egg hunt alone. Oh well, maybe we'll summon our inner Bunnicula and create our own Easterween.

Bookwoman, Bookstore

5501 NORTH LAMAR BOULEVARD, #A-105

Our only regret about visiting Bookwoman is that we didn't give ourselves enough time to peruse the robust selection. A forty-seven-year institution of Austin, this feminist bookstore has moved around the city, starting out with the name Common Woman Bookstore in honor of queer poet Judy Grahn's *The Work of a Common Woman* (1973). A distinctly female and queer space, Bookwoman is what we imagine a bookstore in hippie-era Berkeley might have looked like. Postered with liberal signage, Bookwoman boasts an even larger selection of tarot and oracle cards than the Glass Coffin. Despite the rather small size of the store, the poetry section was overwhelming in the best way. Shopping the horror section was a refreshing change, as Bookwoman carries only female-identifying authors and a smaller selection of books by men that are about women. Meg picked up a copy of the horror novel *No Gods for Drowning* (2022) by Hailey Piper, and her goal for our next visit is to be better versed in poetry so she can confidently shop that slamming poetry section (all puns intended).

Lucky Lizard Curios and Gifts, Collectibles

412 EAST SIXTH STREET

After a walk through Museum of the Weird, you're naturally going to want to get your hands on some zany stuff of your own. Our favorite purchases were alien earrings...You can truly never have enough. There are also Museum of the Weird T-shirts, collectibles, and a lot to look at even if you've run out of money. We suggest that if you don't have time or funds for the museum, at least stop at Lucky Lizard to take in the grandeur of Big Foot and an Audrey II–style carnivorous plant.

WHERE TO STAY

The Driskill Hotel

604 BRAZOS STREET

Yes, it's spelled that way, emphasis on *kill*. Okay, now that we've got that out of our systems, let us paint you a picture of the stunning Driskill Hotel. Amid the historic buildings and rollicking nightlife on the intersection of Sixth Street and Brazos Street, the hotel, built in 1886, stands out. It is a landmark of luxury, a stunning collaboration of Spanish Revival meets Gothic details that's filled with Art Deco touches inside. Charm awaits every corner. There's a restored safe door, propped open so you can sneak inside a cubby. Every larger-than-life painting comes with a plaque explaining its history. Each floor has its own library by the elevators, as well as artifacts encased in glass, reminding us of a time gone by. There is an audio art tour, as well as a guided walk of the hotel in the afternoon, and they provide a fancy tea service that screams Jane Austen.

There's something special in the air at the Driskill. We couldn't help but notice how well-dressed everyone was, like they knew to act proper under the watchful ghosts of former guests.

The Driskill's history is steeped in politics, as it is close to the Texas State Capitol House and was known as the headquarters for President Lyndon B. Johnson's campaign (he also had his first date with Lady Bird in The Driskill Bar). Many political deals, maybe not all super legal, were made under those high ceilings.

Like any building built so long ago, the Driskill has its share of ghost stories. They start with founder Jesse Driskill, who, like a true cowboy, lost his hotel in a poker game shortly after it opened. In her book *True*

Haunted Tales of the Driskill Hotel (2013), Monica Ballard recounts a sighting: "One of my most favorite stories is one of the few sightings we've had of Colonel Driskill. One of his favorite rooms in the Driskill overlooks Sixth Street and Brazos, and there was a consultant in town who woke up one night to see a gentleman standing in his room, looking out the window about three o'clock in the morning, puffing on a cigar. He sat up in bed and said, 'Hey, fella, what the hell are you doing in my room?' He said the guy looked at him and gave him this look, like, *Your room*? But he didn't say anything. The consultant leaned over and snapped on the light by the bed, and when the light came on, there was no one standing by the window, but the curtains were still swaying and there was a cloud of cigar smoke in the air."

Epic. If we come back as ghosts, we hope we have the same cool confidence as Jesse Driskill. There are other ghost sightings, like none other than the presidential Johnsons reliving their courtship, as well as a jilted bride who died by suicide in the hotel. We think the most unnerving ghost is four-year-old Samantha Houston, granddaughter of the famous Sam Houston. Legend has it that little Samantha died from an accidental fall on the Driskill Hotel's grand staircase. She is heard to this day playing with a bouncy ball on the steps and is known also to be spotted near a painting of her likeness on the fifth floor. We've learned from horror movies that little girl ghosts are best to stay away from, so we were happy to stay on the twelfth floor.

WHERE TO EAT

1886 Cafe and Bakery

604 BRAZOS STREET

Pricey but worth it, the 1886 Cafe and Bakery, located in the Driskill, is where to get a one-of-a-kind breakfast. Fuel your goth adventures in this Victorian café, where you can get a cinnamon roll the size of your head. There are also personal chocolate cakes lovingly decorated with "1886" to signify when The Heritage Society, a female-run institution, founded the Lunchroom, known as the "socializing parlor" of its day. Now, the café is a throwback to its Victorian roots. The tall ceiling, stained-glass door, and toile wallpaper all made us feel mighty fancy so early in the morning. Meg ordered the Texas Migas, a dish of scrambled eggs tossed with fresh avocados, caramelized onions, jalapeños, and tortilla strips. Basically, Texas heaven in her mouth. You can also choose from classic huevos rancheros or Texas-shaped Belgian waffles slathered in whipped cream. The aesthetic will make any devotee to the dark feel at home in Victorian grandeur. And the food will make you so full you'll be ready for a packed day experiencing Austin's dark adventures.

Chupacabra Cantina

400 EAST SIXTH STREET

After you've been through the titillating displays at the Museum of the Weird, drop in right next door to Chupacabra Cantina. In Mexico, children have been properly scared poopless by the legend of the cryptid Chupacabra. As for us two Minnesotans, we hadn't heard of the creature until a memorable episode from the fourth season of *The X-Files* (1993–2018) entitled "El Mundo Gira."

FBI agents Mulder and Scully go on the hunt to discover who murdered a Mexican immigrant in California. Locals in her neighborhood believe she was killed by the Chupacabra, which translates to *goat sucker*. It's known to drink the blood from farm animals and, naturally, turn on little children out causing mischief at night. On *The X-Files,* it turns out things are a lot more complicated for Mulder and Scully (an otherworldly fungus is at fault) than any bloodsucking cryptid. Even so, the lore of the Chupacabra has continued to grow its status in media, from horror films like *Indigenous* (2014) to games like Magic: The Gathering, which added a Ravenous Chupacabra card in 2018.

Like its brethren (Big Foot, the Loch Ness Monster), the Chupacabra has long been a creature nestled in the shadows of myth. As reported in *National Geographic*, recent "discoveries" of Chupacabras have proven to be fake. "In almost all these cases, the monsters have turned out to be coyotes suffering from very severe cases of mange."

Okay, so maybe there's no proof that the Chupacabra is stalking Mexico and the American Southwest, but that doesn't mean we can't enjoy a visit to Chupacabra Cantina on historic Sixth Street. The Tex-Mex bar and restaurant properly pays homage to its titular monster with art. Its fanged figure is even on the bathroom signage. There are horror events here too, like the Zombie Prom in October and a spooky Cinco de Mayo celebration. They specialize in huge shareable cocktails with vibrant straws for all, as well as Mexican fare like the aptly named Chupacabra, a barbacoa taco with ghost chile aioli. We think if the goat-sucking cryptid really does exist, she would *for sure* be a fan of Chupacabra Cantina. And just think...she won't even need a straw.

Zombie Taco

2552 GUADALUPE STREET

As we write this in our hotel bar, the taste of the delicious spicy quinoa and cauliflower tacos we had for lunch lingers on our tongues. We had a blast at Zombie Taco, which also has locations in Chicago and Louisville. Along with the nummy tacos, we had chips with fresh guacamole, queso, and tomatillo salsa verde. Tucked into the lobby of the Moxy Hotel on the border of the University of Texas-Austin, Zombie Taco is definitely in the right place to serve its youthful clientele. Just like the trendy Moxy, the restaurant is cleverly decorated with a whimsical attention to detail. Painted zombie hands beckon you in, and one of those frequently-sold-out ten-foot Home Depot skeletons lords over you, grinning down as you chomp on tacos.

Fit for working college students, each little booth is equipped with charging stations. The intimate indoor seating is lovely, lit with found-art light fixtures. The outdoor area was even more enticing, calling us into the sweltering sun with the promise of old-fashioned plank swings, a ping-pong table, Jenga, and fire tables that we assume meant at some point Austin must get cool enough to use. Zombie Taco is super convenient, as it's open twenty-four hours on the weekends. Best part? It's one of the most affordable lunch spots we've visited: three tacos for thirteen (yep, our lucky number) bucks.

A WOMAN YOU SHOULD KNOW

Maddy Newquist

Growing up in the era of those pesky card catalogs, we know how valuable a caring and knowledgeable librarian can be. We celebrate all librarians, especially the ones in school who patiently sorted through piles of books to find the right Roald Dahl or R. L. Stine for us. But what about a librarian who is using her time and talents to promote horror literature? That just brings her to a whole new level of awesomeness. That's why Maddy Newquist, a current librarian at the Austin Public Library, is a woman you should definitely know.

Newquist produces and hosts *APL Volumes*, a podcast where she delves into a different genre every season, especially ones that are often overlooked by libraries, like horror. The first episode focused on Stephen King's *The Shining* (1977) as well as Stanley Kubrick's 1980 film adaptation. As profiled in *Austin Monthly*, "The rest of the season will be divided by horror subgenres such as cosmic, gothic, humor, paranormal, psychological, and visceral. With a new episode every other week, Newquist will explore the works of icons like Poe and H. P. Lovecraft, as well as influential newcomers such as Victor LaValle, T. Kingfisher, and Agustina Bazterrica. Nonwhite, queer, and non-English-speaking authors are a particular focal point."

Thank you, Maddy Newquist, for highlighting books by diverse and horrifically talented authors who more readers need to find.

TRAVEL TIPS

1. Because Austin is a hotbed of artistic expression, make sure you check a festival calendar so you can plan your trip around events like the Final Girl Fest, where fans can meet their favorite "final girls," like Barbara Crampton (*Re-Animator*, 1985) and Rachel True (*The Craft*, 1996).

2. Even in early spring, it was over ninety degrees and muggy. If your hair turns into a tragic mess in such weather (like ours), make sure to pack your products. Or do it like Austin and embrace the weird.

3. Austin is known for its diverse collection of food trucks in nearly every section of the city. They range from Bohemian Barbeque to Crepe Crazy and everything in between. There's even a family-friendly food truck park with a jungle gym and community garden. Check out roaminghunger.com to plan a day eating your way through Austin.

4. The Museum of the Weird makes a suggestion on their website to visit on a weekday, so you have more space and time to look at the exhibits. We agree, as it was tight in some areas, and fewer people is always better!

5. Austin is also known for its street art. Slow down and take a look at such eclectic installations as the Cathedral of Junk or the outside of the Mexic-Arte Museum, which has rotating Latino artists decorate their Fifth Street wall.

OTHER SPOOKY PLACES AROUND THE STATE

Texarkana

The Town That Dreaded Sundown (1976) takes place in Texarkana, Texas, and is based on the true case of a serial killer in 1946. The Texarkana Moonlight Murders were never solved.

Marfa

The Marfa Lights are mysterious orbs that have been appearing since the 1800s in the Marfa area. The city holds an annual festival to celebrate these unexplained phenomena, which appear year-round.

San Antonio

Woman Hollering Creek, located in San Antonio, Texas, is rumored to be home to the legend of La Llorona, the ghost of a woman who drowned her children and now cries and mourns them with her screams.

The historic Alamo in San Antonio, Texas, is considered to be one of the most haunted locations in the state. The Mexican army had reclaimed the Alamo, refusing to take prisoners and choosing to kill all who stood their ground. After thousands were killed in a thirteen-day siege between the Mexican and Texan armies in 1836, their bodies were buried in mass graves. A watershed moment in the Texas Revolution, the Battle of the Alamo was extremely deadly, its significance still resonating today. It's no surprise that security guards have reported seeing ghostly figures wandering at night, and hearing footsteps when no one is around on such contentious ground.

WELCOME TO

NEW YORK CITY

NEW YORK

POPULATION: 8.4 MILLION

SPOOKIEST THING TO HAPPEN HERE

As lifelong horror fans, we've watched our share of creature features with gigantic monsters attacking a town. New York City rats may not be the beasts they're made out to be in films like *Graveyard Shift* (1990) or *The Killer Shrews* (1959), but they can grow to a scary size, and the sheer number of them is frightening.

In 2012, a three-foot-long rodent was found dead in a shoe shop in the Bronx. Experts believe it was a Gambian pouched rat, a common pet—although illegal to own—that is native to Africa. The most common rat found in New York is the brown rat, which isn't as big but is far more prevalent. According to *The Atlantic*, "one study put the real number at about two hundred and fifty thousand [rats] by 1950. By 2014, that had grown to about two million—an eight hundred percent boom in fewer than sixty-five years..."

The rat population has not only grown exponentially; it has also spread. In 1974, another rat survey of New York found that only about eleven percent of the city was rat afflicted. Today, Corrigan puts the estimate at eighty to ninety percent. We saw several rats on the street and in the subway while visiting, but in our opinion, they were cute. (Get back to us when they're menacing us in our own homes, though.) In 2023, New York City hired their first rat czar, Kathleen Corrodi, whose job it is to address the rising rat population.

HIDDEN GEM WE DISCOVERED

Caveat

21A CLINTON STREET

Caveat, a self-proclaimed nerdy comedy venue in Manhattan, is home to multiple shows per week. As *New York Magazine* wrote, "Ben Lillie, a particle physicist and cofounder of science podcast *The Story Collider*, opened Caveat on the Lower East Side to pair drinking and thinking." Stop by to learn about a variety of topics from shows like *The Science of Horror, Nosferatu: In Concert, and My Horror Manifesto*. Grab a snack or cocktail at the bar, take a seat, and be prepared to learn and meet fellow nerds who are interested in learning and laughing together. We had a great time presenting at Caveat and believe in their statement that "life's about learning, and learning's better with jokes."

 There are several ghost tours and haunted tours to take on visits to New York City. Choose between self-guided, walking, and more.

MOST FAMOUS TRUE CRIME

The Amityville Horror (1979) was based on the book of the same name by author Jay Anson. It tells the story of the Lutz family, who were plagued by supernatural happenings in their home and fled the premises after spending only twenty-eight days there. The home, which is located in Amityville, Long Island (about an hour and a half outside of Manhattan), was the site of six murders committed by Ronald DeFeo Jr. in 1974. DeFeo claimed to have heard the voices of his family plotting against him, but his story changed several times after the night of the murders. He was found guilty of six counts of second-degree murder and sentenced to six twenty-five-year sentences. He died in prison in 2021. We visited the house from afar when we traveled to New York, but be aware that the home is privately owned and is not a tourist site.

 ## SPOOKY MOVIES AND BOOKS SET HERE

BOOKS

The Drawing of the Three (1987)
  by Stephen King
Books of Blood (1984, 1985)
  by Clive Barker

MOVIES

Rosemary's Baby (1968)
Friday the 13th Part VIII (1989)
Scream VI (2023)

 # WHAT TO DO

The Edgar Allan Poe Cottage

2640 GRAND CONCOURSE

There comes a moment in every horror lover's life, most likely in those awkward middle-school years, when they are introduced to the macabre works of Edgar Allan Poe. His powerful, descriptive language adorned with rotting corpses, women dressed in Victorian finery, and devices fit for torture speaks to those of us drawn to the dark side. Our first exposure to Poe was his tale of a guilt-ridden murderer in the short story "The Tell-Tale Heart" (1843). A psychological slow burn, the story was a heady experience when we were kids, and it remains an influence on our writing today. After our first reading, we were pretty sure Poe was the most epic horror writer to have ever lived. This belief only intensified as Meg pursued studies in early American gothic literature, steeping herself in all things Poe. The way Poe wrote about death, war, love, *everything*, was through his own unique kaleidoscope of terror, which spurred on Meg's own love of the gory details.

 Meg's favorite Edgar Allan Poe stories: "The Tell-Tale Heart" (1843), "The Murders in the Rue Morgue" (1841), and "The Black Cat" (1843). Kelly's favorite Edgar Allan Poe adaptations: *The Fall of the House of Usher* (2022), *The Pit and the Pendulum* (1961), and *The Masque of the Red Death* (1964).

Fitting for such a master of horror, Poe's life was marked with tragedy, including his mysterious death in 1849 at only forty years old. His cause of death has never been fully explained, with numerous experts weighing in with their guesses ranging from cholera to suicide, as well as a phenomenon called "cooping." This is when people were forced to imbibe deadly amounts of alcohol by gangs so that they could be coerced into voting for a candidate multiple times.

 Poe lived in the Bronx for a time, so we wonder what he would think of *Vampires vs. The Bronx* (2020), a comedy horror movie in which vampires take over the community as an allegory for gentrification.

Before his untimely death, Poe spent time in the Bronx, a borough of New York, in a rental cottage. Built in 1812, it was rented to Poe, his wife, Virginia, and his mother-in-law, Maria, from 1846 to 1849. They moved there to breathe the "fresh country air," hoping it would improve Virginia's health. As we came across the cottage nearly two centuries later, this notion of country life is laughable, as the anachronistic cottage is smack-dab in the middle of numerous buildings. The population has now grown around it to over 1.4 million people.

It was here that Poe wrote poems such as "The Bells" (1849), "Eureka" (1848), and "Annabel Lee" (1849), the last of which has become a popular love poem for those of us who appreciate a sense of impending doom with our romance. It is no wonder that Poe wrote "Annabel Lee" in the cottage, as many believe it was an ode to Virginia, who died of tuberculosis in that very house in 1847. The painful death of a beautiful young woman in the quaint cottage could be pulled from the shadowy depths of Poe's own tales.

 Hart Island is located in the Bronx. It contains New York's Potter's Field, a burial site for unknown individuals. It has also been a burial site for amputated body parts and was home to a women's lunatic asylum, a tubercularium, a corrections facility for delinquent boys, and a Nike missile base.

The cottage now sits next to Poe Park, formerly Highbridge Park, and has been open as a museum since 1913. A thorough and knowledgeable tour guide takes guests through not only the history of the property but the life and times of Edgar Allan Poe.

Eager to begin our gothic journey, we arrived at the cottage's opening at eleven sharp, uncertain which door to go through. The white clapboard house was a unique sight amid the colorful bustle of the Bronx. We were instantly taken with the sense of going back in time, wondering what the grounds must have looked like a century and a half ago. As Kelly took a photo of Meg on the front porch, our hearts ached from the proximity of Poe. He had been a horror mentor to us, someone who pulled back the pretentious curtain of early American literature, exposing what we craved to read and write: the dark, the twisted, and the emotional.

Famous horror icon Vincent Price starred in seven film adaptations of Edgar Allan Poe stories, including *House of Usher* (1960), *Tales of Terror* (1962), and *The Haunted Palace* (1963).

As we entered the cottage for a tour, we couldn't help but be struck by the small size of the home, especially as Poe was at his most successful at the time of the rental. If we lived here, there would be no room for our horror action figures—not to mention our book collections!

With a group of fellow Poe enthusiasts, we were given a lovely tour of the cottage. Our guide, Daryl, not only gave us a great background of biographical and local history but most importantly noticed Meg's Poe raven tattoo! It's nice to have your dark literary interests validated.

Every moment we spent in the house we were hyperaware that Poe had lived inside those very walls. It was as if his heart was beating beneath the floorboards, a throbbing reminder of the past. We thought about Virginia, how she had lost her life inside that very house, a watershed moment for Poe that would go on to inspire a sullen turn in his work.

Nevermore: The Imaginary Life and Mysterious Death of Edgar Allan Poe is a 2014 musical written and composed by Jonathan Christenson. Listen to our *Horror Rewind* podcast episode to hear about our experience seeing the musical live in Minnesota.

Staged as it would've been in Poe's residence, the cottage has some original furniture, including a writing desk. Knowing that Poe himself had touched these items, sat at that very desk, and written his masterpieces there gave us an undeniable thrill. It was as though we had been drawn into some portal between the past and the present. In every corner, we lingered, touching what we could, like wood moldings and gilded picture frames. It was equally as fun to watch the reactions of those on the tour with us, as everyone had been touched by Poe's words before finding themselves in this seemingly time-forgotten cottage in the Bronx.

As our tour wound down, we were escorted upstairs to the attic space, where a documentary played. While this was informative, the guide and tour downstairs held more interest. Meg found herself eager to get back to the heart of the home, hoping maybe she could breathe in Poe's essence.

Before we left, we made sure to check out the modest gift shop. Meg still has her pewter Poe key chain to remind her of the day we stood within the space that had once held such horror genius.

One point of knowledge we learned was that while living in the Bronx, formerly known as the Village of Fordham, Poe would take walks throughout the neighborhood. One of his favorite jaunts was walking over the High Bridge. This is the oldest bridge in New York City, having been completed in 1848. After touring the cottage and park, you can take this three-mile walk to the High Bridge. Picture yourself strolling like Poe did, finding inspiration for your next spooky tale!

As we walked the same route as Poe, we reveled in the beauty of our surroundings. Yes, a lot has changed, but the grassy park, fallen leaves, and rainy day made for appropriate gothic vibes. Even the wrought iron spindles around the park, and Highbridge itself, could've been sketched in an illustrated "The Fall of the House of Usher" (1839). Leaving the cottage and its area in the Bronx was not easy, as we had felt as though we were in a goth girl's fever dream, taking in the soul of Edgar Allan Poe through his environs.

Woodlawn Cemetery
4199 WEBSTER AVENUE

A day of creepy sights is not complete until we hit up a local graveyard. We continued to have the perfect cloudy atmosphere for our late-afternoon self-guided walk around Woodlawn Cemetery. There are impressive mausoleums and statues that would look at home on any Roger Corman set of a Poe film adaptation. Though we weren't there for a formal tour, Woodlawn offers many options, including a Woodlawn Women Who Made a Difference Trolley Tour and a Lecture and Scavenger Hunt on the Egyptian Iconography at Woodlawn. These tours and events vary in price from free up to $25.

Thankfully, as we took in our surroundings, the cemetery's website has a detailed listing of its impressive residents, including a page devoted to women who left an indelible mark on history.

Our first stop was at the tomb with a name we instantly recognized: Nellie Bly (1864–1922). Bly was considered the first investigative journalist. She infiltrated a mental institution in order to expose its sexist, racist, and overall demeaning practices. Her book *Ten Days in a Madhouse* (1887) is a disturbing account of her time as a patient. It's a recommended read that starkly details what it was to be a woman in nineteenth-century New York. Standing at her final resting place was a sobering reminder of the women before us who worked tirelessly to have their writing and, most poignantly, their existence taken seriously. It left us shaken for a moment, to be at her feet, and then inspired to continue her legacy of making women's voices heard.

Another notable grave at Woodlawn is that of author Herman Melville (1819–1891). He is best known for his classic novel about a man looking to vanquish a white whale, *Moby-Dick* (1851), but our personal favorite is his short story "Bartleby, the Scrivener" (1853). Every fan of the macabre should give this story a read, as it embraces a rebellious spirit with a bit of high strangeness. In fact, the character Bartleby utters one of our favorite literary quotes that resonates with introverts: "I'd prefer not to." As self-proclaimed "literature nerds," we felt it was an honor to stand at Melville's grave on that autumn afternoon. Just as with our experience at Poe's cottage, we felt an almost indescribable tingle at being so close to such an icon.

We recommend you perhaps bring a copy of "Bartleby" you purchased from The Lit. Bar bookstore in the Bronx and read it upon Melville's grave for maximum goth vibes. Don't forget a gauzy black blanket to drape across the dead leaves.

Sleepy Hollow

A little over an hour north of New York City lies a village originally known as North Tarrytown. Made famous by Washington Irving's story "The Legend of Sleepy Hollow" (1920), the town took on its new name in 1996. The author is buried in the Sleepy Hollow Cemetery, and there are plenty of other sites to see, including

shops, the Headless Horseman Bridge, the Philipsburg Manor Museum, and a sculpture of the Headless Horseman. The town, which is home to about ten thousand people, comes alive in the fall with a festival called the Great Jack-O-Lantern blaze, featuring over seven thousand illuminated hand-carved pumpkins. There are other activities, like a haunted hayride and a Halloween 10K run. We had a lovely time strolling through the village, enjoying lunch at a local tavern, and picking up some souvenirs to remember our visit by.

Madame Tussauds Wax Museum

234 WEST FORTY-SECOND STREET

The Warner Bros. Icons of Horror exhibit is included with every admission ticket to Madame Tussauds. You'll see horror icons from movies like *The Nun* (2018) and *Annabelle* (2014) to Pennywise from *It* (2017). As with all wax figures, we get thoroughly creeped out by their realism—and seeing a horror villain looking directly at you? Bone chilling. The museum also includes a Marvel Hall of Fame, a *Ghostbusters* (2016) exhibit, and a face-off with King Kong.

Broadway

When you're in New York City, you must attend a Broadway show. On one of our visits, we had the opportunity to attend *Beetlejuice* the musical at its original home on Broadway at the Winter Garden Theatre. Based on the 1988 film, the musical follows the Deetz family as they move into a house inhabited by the ghosts of its former owners.

It was fun to see how beloved the movie and characters were to a sold-out crowd. The energy and excitement when the show began were palpable. The plot deviates a bit from the film but does so in a way to build backstory and character arcs for Lydia and her stepmother. Beetlejuice's character is a bit different as well and works more with Lydia as a team than as a manipulator. He's still a cheeky villain, but this time he sings and dances too!

Stop by the gift shop during intermission or after the show to pick up your own copy of *The Handbook for the Recently Deceased* or a fun commemorative T-shirt to put out the goth vibes to fellow fans. Whether you can make it to *Beetlejuice* or not, attend some live theater while you're in New York City. It's an experience you'll never forget!

 There have been numerous horror musicals on Broadway over the years, including *Sweeney Todd* (1979), *American Psycho* (2013), *The Addams Family* (2009), and *The Toxic Avenger* (2008).

WHERE TO STAY

Waldorf Astoria

301 PARK AVENUE

Although we have often crashed with friends when traveling to New York City, we've also ventured out to check out convenient and sometimes haunted hotels. The Waldorf Astoria, located on Park Ave., is undergoing renovations and will reopen in 2025. When we stayed there before it was closed, we loved exploring the 1931 Art Deco–style property and Grand Central Station nearby. At the train station, you'll find a platform with a secret entrance and elevator that once led straight into the hotel. Some say President Franklin D. Roosevelt used the entrance and still haunts it today with his dog Fala. If you hear barking, you'll know who it is.

Library Hotel

299 MADISON AVENUE

Imagine a hotel with a twenty-four-hour reading room, access to over six thousand books, and refreshments at your fingertips. You don't have to imagine it, because it exists on Madison Avenue in New York. Each of the ten floors is dedicated to one of the ten major categories of the Dewey Decimal Classification, including social sciences, literature, languages, history, math and science, general knowledge, technology, philosophy, the arts, and religion. You can even request a theme, and the hotel will do their best to accommodate you in the room that has been curated with books and art relevant to the corresponding topic. The Library Hotel is full of quaint and comfortable sitting areas that you can share alone or with fellow book lovers, and the location is convenient for all your sightseeing needs. We recommend going on a horror book hunt while on site to find all the classics by Shelley and Poe. With an on-site restaurant and rooftop bar, you may never want to leave.

WHERE TO EAT

Beetle House

308 EAST SIXTH STREET

Our next stop in New York was Beetle House, the Tim Burton–themed restaurant, where every day is Halloween. Reservations are recommended as the space is quite cozy.

Featuring dark and creepy-themed drinks and food, this is a must-stop for every goth. From the *Beetlejuice* (1988) tombstone above the bar to the fun decor covering every wall, Beetle House had us smiling from ear to ear. As lifelong Tim Burton fans, we were instantly pleased to be a small part of his phantasmagoric world. Feeling like we were two Lydia Deetzes traversing the many settings of *Charlie and the Chocolate Factory* (2005), *Edward Scissorhands* (1990), and *Nightmare before Christmas* (1993), we were in black-and-white-striped heaven! Resplendent under the purple haze, we had finally been given the golden ticket.

We couldn't help but think of our younger selves, who would've fainted at the thought of such a place ever existing. We began with a round of drinks: the This Is Halloween cocktail, which consisted of cinnamon liquor, sour apple Pucker, pumpkin liqueur, apple cider, and ginger beer, was a hit, as was the Beetle's Juice, made with tequila, muddled blackberry, and cranberry juice. The menu has numerous ghoulish options with fun names like Edward Burger Hands as well as Frites and Frights, and make sure to save some room for dessert or another round of drinks. Workers dressed as characters from Tim Burton films interact with guests and stay in character throughout the exchanges. Beetlejuice proved to live up to his filmic counterpart, as he was quite pushy. He often came to our table to do some prop comedy, which...um...was funnier in the movie!

A light rain was falling as we left Beetle House, and we felt like we were cast in a Tim Burton film written by Edgar Allan Poe. It had been a scare-coaster of a day, with high loops of emotion, unexpected twists of rain and, in the end, such a grand feeling of gothic accomplishment.

Flying Fox Tavern

678 WOODWARD AVENUE

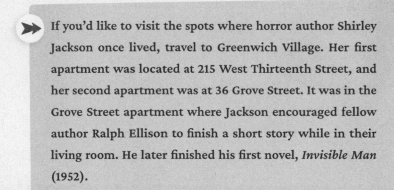

If you're in the Ridgewood Queens area, stop by Flying Fox Tavern for a bite and a drink. The gothic feel of the tavern is accented by the names of the cocktails, including Nosferatu, Vampira, Christopher Lee, and the Count. With movie nights, watch parties, and other events to benefit local nonprofits, we were thrilled to spend an evening at the Flying Fox.

> If you'd like to visit the spots where horror author Shirley Jackson once lived, travel to Greenwich Village. Her first apartment was located at 215 West Thirteenth Street, and her second apartment was at 36 Grove Street. It was in the Grove Street apartment where Jackson encouraged fellow author Ralph Ellison to finish a short story while in their living room. He later finished his first novel, *Invisible Man* (1952).

WHERE TO SHOP

The Lit. Bar, Bookstore

131 ALEXANDER AVENUE

Next stop? What would Edgar Allan Poe do? Let's get some books! Also in the neighborhood of the Bronx is the Lit. Bar. This is the only independent bookstore in the borough and was opened by Noelle Santos in 2019. Santos sees the bookstore as a way to cater to a community that is often underserved in publishing. As she told *Black Enterprise* in 2020, "It was important to me to not be the 'Black bookstore.' It's important that it's Black-owned, but I made sure to have books not only for people of color but for people with disabilities, LGBTQ communities, and the older generation." Peruse the books and enjoy a glass of wine as you read the fiction or nonfiction of your choosing.

After our surreal experience at the Poe cottage, in which we felt as though we had been transported to the past, the Lit. Bar was a refreshing welcome back to the twenty-first century. A few mimosas and a perusal through the ample horror section helped restore us for the rest of our horror-infused journey.

Abracadabra NYC, Collectibles

19 WEST TWENTY-FIRST STREET

If you're looking for toys, collectibles, costumes, and more, stop by Abracadabra NYC. Not only is the shop fun to browse through for yourself, but you may also run into a professional scouting props or costumes for TV, movies, print, or theater productions. They have a nice selection of horror collectibles, action figures, and ornaments, and once again, we debated buying more luggage to bring home all the items we wanted to purchase.

 # A WOMAN YOU SHOULD KNOW

Nia DaCosta

(1989–)

Born in Brooklyn, New York in 1989, Nia DaCosta has already accomplished more than most so far in her career. DaCosta was the first Black female director to have a film debut at the top of the box office, with the supernatural horror-slasher film *Candyman* in 2021. It was also announced that she was hired to direct *The Marvels* (2023), making her the youngest filmmaker to ever direct a Marvel movie and the first African American woman. In a 2021 interview with *Esquire* DaCosta said, "I think all horror movies are about trauma in one way or another, but I would love for there to be more space even within horror for us to talk about stuff that's not 'Being Black is really sad'... There are so many facets to our existence." We can't wait to see what she does next with her career.

 Fans of Stephen King's *Dark Tower* series (1992–2012) should visit Second Avenue and Forty-Sixth Street in New York City to see the fictional location of the rose from the books.

TRAVEL TIPS

1. Goth pro-tip: Keep those studded boots at home for most excursions in New York City. There's lots of walking, so opt instead for your skull high-tops. Also remember to pack a raincoat for light drizzle depending on the time of year you visit.

2. Attractions that are considered "touristy" are sometimes worth visiting. The Empire State Building offers a glorious view of the city and is a must-see. Pretend you're Fay Wray in *King Kong* (1933) and take in the sights. We recommend going early in the morning or late at night on a weekday to avoid the crowds.

3. Another popular tourist destination in New York that is worth visiting is Ellis Island. Over twelve million immigrants entering the United States were processed on the island, and several thousand died upon entry. Visitors and workers alike claim to have experienced ghostly encounters while visiting Ellis Island. We recommend exploring the exhibits to read the history and about the incredible individuals who came through the building.

4. There are several airport choices: Newark (EWR), John F. Kennedy (JFK), and LaGuardia (LGA). Check train schedules to go to and from the airport, and plan ahead for potential delays. Depending on the amount of baggage we have, sometimes we choose a rideshare or taxi option over the hassle of lugging our items up and down subway steps.

5. Don't be afraid to take a bus tour of New York City. We've gone on several and have seen so much more than we could have reached on our own. It's also nice to sit back, relax, and let an expert inform you about where you are and what you are seeing. We recommend planning it early in your trip so you can revisit any place you feel you didn't get to spend enough time seeing.

DULUTH

MINNESOTA

POPULATION: 86,372

SPOOKIEST THING TO HAPPEN HERE

An Indigenous legend, the Wendigo is known as an evil spirit that devours mankind. Stories of the creature lurking in the Northwoods of Minnesota include descriptions of it being over fifteen feet tall and having glowing eyes, yellow fangs, and an insatiable hunger for human flesh. Some people believe that a Wendigo is created when a human resorts to cannibalism for survival—a harsh truth that occurred during past Minnesota winters. The legend also lends its name to the modern medical term *Wendigo psychosis*. "Some psychiatrists consider it a syndrome that creates an intense craving for human flesh and a fear of becoming a cannibal. Ironically, this psychosis occurs in people living around the Great Lakes of Canada and the United States." Wendigo psychosis usually developed in individuals who are isolated by heavy snow for a long period of time and presented with initial symptoms of poor appetite, nausea, and vomiting. The person could also develop a delusion of being transformed into a Wendigo and seeing others as a food source. Reports of this psychosis date back to the 1600s.

HIDDEN GEM WE DISCOVERED

Jade Fountain Cocktail Lounge

305 NORTH CENTRAL AVENUE

Jade Fountain in Duluth's Spirit Valley neighborhood is an eclectic and fun spot to grab drinks before dinner or a movie. Originally opened in 1968, Jade Fountain was a Chinese restaurant and bar that operated for more than forty years. New ownership turned the restaurant into a bar and lounge that features much of the original decor, tiki bar–style drinks, beaded doorways, and perfect lighting for a ghouls' night out. We enjoyed mai tais and wine in classic vintage glassware while we toured the numerous decorations throughout the space. While there, you'll be steps away from the West Theatre, an Art Deco venue that opened in 1937; locally owned Zenith Bookstore; and Wussow's Concert café, a coffeehouse that offers coffee, food, alcohol, and entertainment.

MOST FAMOUS TRUE CRIME

On the shores of Lake Superior sits a magnificently beautiful mansion flanked by towering pines. There is a small cemetery with an appropriately gothic wrought iron fence, a horse stable, and views of the tempestuous lake from nearly every angle. Glensheen Mansion is now owned by the University of Minnesota Duluth, but it was the family home of the Congdons for seventy years, starting in 1908.

Taking a tour of the thirty-nine-room mansion is an unforgettable experience. You're able to see in authentic detail how the Congdon family lived. Just, whatever you do, *don't* ask about the murders. The tour guides will not answer questions regarding the darkest day of Glensheen's history: June 27, 1977.

On that night the elderly Elisabeth Congdon was killed in her bed, and her nurse, Velma Pietila, was left lifeless on the staircase. It was soon discovered they had been killed, for the popular motive of money, by Congdon's own son-in-law Roger Caldwell. Although it was believed the daughter Marjorie was also involved, she was not convicted.

If you're interested in learning more about Duluth's most notorious murders, we suggest you check out the play *Glensheen*, which hasn't stopped its run at the History Theatre in St. Paul, Minnesota. If you'd rather sit on Glensheen's property and read a book in the lush gardens, then try out *Will to Murder: The True Stories behind the Crimes and Trials Surrounding the Glensheen Killings* (2009) by Gail Feichtinger. If that isn't quick enough, and you're a big fan of cheesy reenactments, then check out the episode "Mystery in the Mansion" of the show *Power, Privilege, and Justice* (2002–) for the full TV true-crime treatment.

Despite the murder, or perhaps because of it, Glensheen Mansion is a thriving tourist destination in Duluth. We've enjoyed sunsets on the property while drinking local brews, as well as art shows. (Meg's mom set up her watercolors there when Meg was a teen. Meg was just as morbidly obsessed with the mansion then, searching for murder clues.) The mansion also hosts sunset snowshoeing and kid-friendly pumpkin hunts. Just whatever you do...keep your murder questions to yourself.

SPOOKY MOVIES AND BOOKS SET HERE

BOOKS

Duma Key (2008) by
    Stephen King

Daughters of the Lake (2018)
    by Wendy Webb

Anoka (2020) by Shane Hawke

MOVIES

You'll Like My Mother (1972)

Jennifer's Body (2009)

I'm Not a Serial Killer (2016)

 # WHAT TO DO

The Lakewalk

ENTRANCES FROM CANAL PARK THROUGH THE LAKESIDE NEIGHBORHOOD

We encourage all our fiendish friends to visit their own backyards with fresh eyes. Growing up in Minnesota, Kelly was fascinated in the first grade by the tale of Big Foot. Her teacher told the students the story of the hairy beast, and Kelly went home that day to explore the woods behind her home. She hasn't found him yet but is intrigued by the notion that creatures could be lurking among us. Meg moved to Minnesota in junior high, and we both became enthralled with all things horror, science, history, and true crime.

By taking a walk along Duluth's Lakewalk, you'll view the lake, forests, and neighborhoods of this harbor city. Lake Superior, the largest freshwater lake on the planet, also holds many of its own secrets. From shipwrecks to sea creature legends, the lake is known for "not giving up her dead." Over 350 shipwrecks took place on the Great Lake, and over half of them still lie undiscovered.

Lake Superior is also known for having some underwater creatures living in it. A first responder to the presumed drowning death of Matthew Bruin in 1987 said: "People say, 'It's the Presque Isle monster' or 'It's a sea serpent,' but it is the lake itself, a force of nature that does not care if we live or die." But the victim's friend and witness J. R. Sandvik said, "I'm telling you he was pulled under by a large animal." Another witness to a death in 2005 recalled:

I heard a thrumming sound, a guttural vibration I associated with an outboard motor sputtering on its way to starting up... This sound was more like a pick of bone strumming thick tendons. It was biological and contained menace. Something heavy and fast bumped against me[;] at first I thought maybe it was a dead tree pushed by the current. Whatever it was, grabbed my buddy and ran with him... My skin had been pierced, stabbed, leaving a searing puncture wound. We had cast ourselves into the stream like bait.

What could explain these attacks? There are several known large species of fish that live in Lake Superior, which include sturgeons that can grow over six feet long, weigh over one hundred pounds, and live to be over one hundred years old. Sturgeons have been known to attack humans when they feel threatened but are also considered gentle giants because they have no teeth. Other fish that reside in the lake are muskies, which can grow up to fifty-eight inches long and weigh up to fifty-five pounds. There have been reports of muskies attacking humans and leaving them with scars and a terrifying story to tell.

Don't let these stories deter you from enjoying the peacefulness and absolute beauty of the lake and surrounding trails. There are sandy beaches on Park Point, past Duluth's iconic lift bridge, and rock beaches farther up the shore. Enjoy the scenery and report back if you do spot or experience anything on your travels.

Nopeming Sanatorium

2650 NOPEMING ROAD

When entering Duluth, you'll see a large abandoned sanatorium on the northbound lane of Interstate 35. Nopeming was built in the early 1900s as a place for patients suffering from tuberculosis and ended as a nursing home in 2002. Its location was chosen for its proximity to Duluth and for the nice, fresh air it offered patients. Paranormal activity has been reported on the abandoned property over the past twenty years and includes people seeing shadow figures in the tunnels and hearing disembodied laughter, moaning, screaming, and other unexplained noises. It is not currently open to the public, but sources say it's possible to arrange tours via the owners. We visited the sanatorium only once and wisely chose not to trespass. Just viewing the land and building from a distance, in the dark, was enough to give us a feeling of dread. As with many of our tours and travels, there is a shift of energy and feelings in places where people have died. We honor their lives and never want to disrespect their memory.

The Depot

506 WEST MICHIGAN STREET

Arguably, one of the best-kept secret haunted places in Duluth for people to visit is the Depot. Opened in 1892, the Duluth Union Depot served "seven railroads with fifty trains arriving and departing each day. The Union Station housed the railroad offices, a newsstand, barber shop, parcel room, and lunchroom. The building was a bustling hub that connected Duluth to the rest of the country." Immigrants from all over the world traveled through the train station in the early 1900s, and it played a vital role in World Wars I and II. The Depot was declared a National Historic Site in 1970, saving it from being demolished, and reopened its doors in 1973 as the St. Louis County Heritage and Arts Center.

Touring the Depot with museum professional Hailey Eidenschink, we heard tales that literally gave us goose bumps, and we could feel the energy shift in places. Reported ghost tales in the building include a curator at the museum who felt a rush of cold air and then saw a little girl dressed in clothing from the 1890s. The girl was looking up at something on a shelf, then disappeared. Years later, the museum received a letter and photos from a woman who had held her wedding reception at the location. A girl appeared in one of the photos, crouching against the wall in the Great Hall. It stood out to the bride because they had not had any children attend their wedding. We stood in the spot where the little girl was crouching and saw the photographic evidence. It was terrifying!

Another space that gave us feelings of heaviness was the immigrant shower room. Enclosed in brick, the room has a single window high above the benches. At night, the darkness can make it feel even creepier. Hailey explained that paranormal experts believe that spirits could be haunting the Depot because of all the immigrants who came through the station, the collection of donated objects like wedding dresses and other mementos, and the large volume of caskets that were transported after someone died and their body was shipped elsewhere for burial.

Perhaps the most haunting tale we heard was of a supposed "Tall Man" spotted in the Great Hall and nearby areas. Someone working at a building across the street from the Depot noticed a man looking out the second-story window one evening after the museum was closed. He thought nothing of it until a few weeks later, when he attended a wedding in the space and noticed there was no second level by the windows where he saw the figure. While touring, we also spotted handprints that were too high to be made by an average-size person standing on the ground. We were immediately spooked. Whether you experience something eerie or not in the Depot, you'll be amazed by the history and stories surrounding you there. Sign up for haunted tours in the month of October or by appointment the rest of the year.

If you're visiting in the fall, make sure to book your ticket on the Terror Train. Taking off from the Depot, the Terror Train is an adults-only costume party, which includes a three-hour excursion up the shore of Lake Superior with live music, a DJ, and libations aboard. There's an optional drop-off in Canal Park for a "zombie crawl" to bars throughout the area. Riding on the historic train is a treat on its own, but to experience an evening with fellow Halloween lovers? Priceless.

William A. Irvin Museum

350 HARBOR DRIVE

If you're visiting Duluth around Halloween, you'll be able to buy a ticket to the Haunted Ship, complete with actors in costume, set pieces, and music to give you a haunted house experience on a historic vessel. But you don't need to visit in the fall to tour the ship and experience some possible ghost sightings.

Launched in 1937 and now listed on the National Register of Historic Places, the *William A. Irvin* is docked on Duluth's waterfront and functions now as a museum. Many people have claimed to see ghosts on board, not during the haunted ship season, and some reports correlate to deaths that took place in history. The most common sighting is of a lady in white period clothing walking around the ship. Others report spotting a captain overseeing the docked ship, while some say they've seen a man who appears to have died after falling from a ladder. Whether you experience a ghost sighting or not, the ship is a stunning display of history and the power of the Great Lakes.

 About an hour north of Duluth, you can explore Minnesota's Iron Range. It has museums, nature, and even an underground mine in Soudan, which will take you half a mile down into the earth. It is also home to one of Minnesota's largest winter hibernation spots for bats and contains between ten thousand and fifteen thousand of them until late June and July.

Duluth's Cemeteries

VARIOUS LOCATIONS

There are several cemeteries in Duluth to visit, including Calvary Cemetery, located on Howard Gnesen Road in Duluth; it was established in 1890 and has recorded over twenty-two thousand burials to date. Some people say you will see floating lights in the cemetery and spirits that haunt their graves if you visit at dusk. Forest Hill Cemetery on Woodland Avenue has had sightings of spirits wandering around houses nearby. Greenwood Cemetery off Rice Lake Road is unmarked and has nearly five thousand people buried in a mass grave. The people include tuberculosis patients, immigrant miners, and lumberjacks. Scandia Cemetery, next to Glensheen Mansion, was established in 1881 and overlooks Lake Superior. As with many older cemeteries, grave markers often sink or disappear entirely due to encroachment by surrounding woods. Volunteers from the Twin Ports Genealogical Society go into cemeteries every summer to clean and repair gravestones. To do this work, it's important to note that you should receive proper training and be given permission from the graveyard manager at whichever location you plan to volunteer.

 Across the bridge, in Superior, Wisconsin, you can tour Fairlawn Mansion. The forty-two-room mansion was built in 1889 and has annual flashlight tours on every Friday the thirteenth. The historic Victorian house is rumored to be haunted by a servant girl who assists guests before she disappears. At least she's helpful.

Enger Tower

1605 ENGER TOWER DRIVE

One of the most iconic structures in Duluth is Enger Tower, which is an eighty-foot-tall, five-story observation tower on top of Enger Hill. A local legend involves a man who jumped headfirst off the fifth level of the tower in 1948. He died upon impact and was never identified. People speculate that this may be why he feels bound to the place where he died. Those who visit Enger Tower have reported seeing a man on the fifth level, but he disappears before they reach him. The tower is lit up in honor of major events throughout the year and provides panoramic views of the city. Bring a lunch or snack to enjoy while visiting, and make sure to clean up after yourselves.

WHERE TO SHOP

The Bookstore at Fitger's, Bookstore

600 EAST SUPERIOR STREET

If you're looking for a fun bookstore in Duluth, we recommend the Bookstore at Fitger's, a charming, fully stocked shop overlooking Lake Superior. Their collection of books features all the current bestsellers as well as classics, books by local authors, and an assortment of gifts. We have never left the store empty-handed and have been thrilled to sign books for readers and fellow horror fans there in the past.

Duluth Tattoo Company, Tattoo Parlor

4504 GRAND AVENUE

Our favorite place to get tattoos in Duluth is the Duluth Tattoo Company. Joshua Kirkpatrick established the shop in 2023, having previously worked at Living Art Studio, where we got numerous tattoos over the years. Kelly's Bates Motel tattoo, designed and inked by Kirkpatrick, even won an award at Minnesota's Crypticon festival for best tattoo! We got our matching Grady Girls from *The Shining* (1980) inked and designed by him as well and still receive endless compliments on them when we're out in public. Schedule your tattoo in advance and tell Josh that Meg and Kelly say hi.

Lady Ocalot's Emporium, Witch Shop

31 WEST SUPERIOR STREET

While we were researching witchcraft for one of our books, we discovered Lady Ocalot's Emporium and became instant fans of the shop. Located in downtown Duluth, the store is your go-to one-stop shop for witchcraft supplies, palm and tarot readings, books, and collectibles. Lorene Couture has been running the shop since September of 2007 and says she's "always been a witch." Couture was raised practicing magic and witchcraft by her mother and continues to practice in and outside of the Emporium. We purchased numerous candles, some incredible jewelry, and other items from the shop. Check the hours, and make an appointment in advance if you'd like a tarot or palm reading.

Hucklebeary, Gift Shop

218 EAST SUPERIOR STREET

Downtown you'll find a shop in the arts district called Hucklebeary. Named after its rescue-mutt mascot, Bear, Hucklebeary is a great place to go for gifts, cards, balloons, and other special treats. Founded by University of Minnesota Duluth alum Emily Ekstrom, the store hopes to inspire people to create and give unique gifts to loved ones. There's even a monthly card club (curated by Bear himself!) that allows members to receive a collection of greeting cards, a free gift, and something fun in the mail every month. Stop by to hopefully get a high five or kiss from Bear and pick up a souvenir to remind you of Duluth.

WHERE TO STAY

Fitger's Inn

600 EAST SUPERIOR STREET

Located in the historic, renovated 1885 Fitger's Brewery, Fitger's Inn is listed on the National Register of Historic Places. Guests are within walking distance of the Lakewalk, Canal Park, numerous restaurants, and Duluth's first microbrewery. With many rooms having fantastic views of the lake, Fitger's Inn is an excellent place to stay while you're visiting the city. We've spent numerous hours in the complex shopping, eating, and attending events, and enjoyed staying at the hotel as a staycation to work on projects and get some much-needed time away from home.

Lake Superior Brewing Brewtel

5324 EAST SUPERIOR STREET

Located in the Lakeside neighborhood, a short drive from downtown Duluth, Lake Superior Brewing has opened a "brewtel." Choose from a two-bedroom apartment, a studio unit, or a three-bedroom house on the Lakewalk for your stay. The restaurant features food for vegans and meat eaters alike, local brews, brick-oven pizzas, and house-made desserts. Having opened in 2022, Lake Superior Brewing is a welcome addition to a mostly residential neighborhood on Duluth's east side. Booking this for your vacation will give you a nice taste of living in a quiet neighborhood in Duluth away from the hustle and bustle of the Canal Park area.

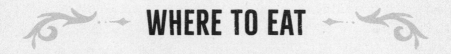

WHERE TO EAT

Apostle Supper Club

505 WEST SUPERIOR STREET

One of our favorite places to dine in Duluth is the Apostle Supper Club. Atop the Radisson hotel, it's Minnesota's only rooftop revolving restaurant. With an atmosphere of a 1960s supper club, the Apostle boasts a full bar with vintage cocktails, an impressive menu, and excellent service. As one of the only fifteen revolving restaurants in the country, this spot is a great place to watch the sun set over the city of Duluth and beautiful Lake Superior. Order a full spate of appetizers, drinks, and dinner, and dessert or an after-dinner drink to savor the night and the experience of this one-of-a-kind restaurant. We highly recommend making reservations.

Zeitgeist

222 EAST SUPERIOR STREET

Another favorite stop of ours is the Zeitgeist complex on Superior Street, which includes a restaurant, bar, movie theater, art gallery, and performance venue all under one roof. Their mission states: "We are a nonprofit arts and community development organization committed to growing and sustaining a community that is inclusive, diverse, and equitable, artistic and vibrant, environmentally conscious, and a place where every individual can thrive. Working in partnership across our region, Zeitgeist connects like-minded organizations and people to collaboratively create programs that make lasting change."

We have been able to see so many horror-themed theater events at Zeitgeist over the years, including *Lizzie the Musical*, *The Birds*, and *Murder Ballad*. If you're in town on a Friday night, watch an independent movie at the Zinema downstairs and then get a ticket for *Renegade Improv*, a hilarious and interactive show in the *teatro*. Since it's located in Duluth's Arts District, you'll be able to attend other shows across the street at the Norshor, have drinks in Blackwater, or throw axes and have a beer at Blacklist.

Bent Paddle

1832 WEST MICHIGAN STREET

There are numerous breweries, cideries, and distilleries in Duluth, all worth visiting in our opinion. We took a behind-the-scenes tour of Bent Paddle in Duluth's Lincoln Park neighborhood; the brewery was opened in 2013 and is owned by two couples. Not only does Bent Paddle feature craft beers, but it also has a Cann-a-Lounge to enjoy CBD and THC sparkling waters and more. We learned on the tour that "the brewers of Bent Paddle Brewing Co. use the amazing water of Lake Superior to brew the freshest and most dependable craft beer and hemp-derived cannabis beverages possible. Lake Superior is ten percent of the world's fresh surface water and one hundred percent of our products are made with that water. It is incredibly soft and mimics the water of Pilsen, Czech Republic, the birthplace of Pilsners." Seeing the production line of cans getting filled with beer reminded us of *Willy Wonka and the Chocolate Factory* (1971), and we were impressed with all the equipment and work that goes into brewing. With their Paddle It Forward initiative, they have donated over $500,000 to nonprofits since opening.

The Rathskeller

132 EAST SUPERIOR STREET

Stop by the Rathskeller for a craft cocktail beneath Superior Street. The bar, which is in Duluth's original 1889 city hall, has a speakeasy feel and a mysterious atmosphere. We've enjoyed numerous nights listening to live music, visiting with friends, and trying unique drinks in the establishment. The Olive Inn, located just above the bar, offers an unforgettable stay with rooms named and themed after historic Duluth figures. Several rooms have cocktails named after them in the bar, allowing you to experience even more of the history and story behind the building. The bar has plenty of non-alcoholic options, an extensive bourbon and scotch list, and local beers. With comfortable seating and dim lighting, the Rathskeller has become a favorite spot to end the night.

The Minnesota Film Festival takes place annually in Duluth and features films from artists all around the world. There are plenty of entertainment options, including a horror shorts block, a sci-fi block, and an Indigenous filmmaker's block. Meet filmmakers and other artists over the five-day event. Their mission states they are passionate about showing films that have been made in small communities, outside of Hollywood or New York, with various budgets. It's the perfect way to get connected to others' stories, perspectives, and art.

A WOMAN YOU SHOULD KNOW

Diablo Cody
(1978–)

Known for her witty, quick dialogue, Diablo Cody is an Academy Award–winning writer and producer who lived in Minnesota and set several of her movies there. Being a lover of horror movies, Diablo wrote 2009's *Jennifer's Body* and set it in the fictional town of Devil's Kettle. The real Devil's Kettle is a waterfall that sits above Lake Superior near Grand Marais, Minnesota, and features a spooky anomaly of the water disappearing from sight as it appears to enter solid rock. We idolize Diablo not only for being from the state we call home but for writing complicated, imperfect female characters. As she told *The Guardian* in 2018, "The expectations [on] women are out of control... I can't believe the disdain towards women who have 'let themselves go.' Why can't I? I'm taking care of three small children; why am I also supposed to be skinny and hot?" She also did a script revision for the reboot of *Evil Dead* (2011) and wrote Lisa Frankenstein (2024), a horror comedy.

 Alice Dougherty, born in Minneapolis, Minnesota, in 1887, was known as one of the few people in the United States to suffer from "werewolf syndrome." She had hair covering her body from head to toe and joined the circus as part of the freak show.

TRAVEL TIPS

1. You can fly directly into Duluth, but if you prefer, you can fly into the Minneapolis/St. Paul airport—about two and a half hours from Duluth—and spend a day or two exploring the Twin Cities. While there, take a ghost tour, visit Prince's Paisley Park in Chanhassen, or battle a true horror: the crowds at the Mall of America. On the drive up to Duluth, you'll pass several interesting haunts, including the Dead End Haunted Hayride in Wyoming, Minnesota; the historic Grant House Hotel in Rush City; and the old Moose Lake School, which is purported to be haunted.

2. While we live in Minnesota and don't mind the cold and snow (most of the time), we recommend traveling here during the summer and autumn months. With below-zero temperatures and possible travel delays due to snowstorms, winter becomes a tricky time to guarantee travel plans in our state. But then again, some of the best horror stories begin with characters stuck in a blizzard!

3. While most places in and around Duluth are accessible by rideshare, renting a car will allow you more opportunities to venture up the North Shore, to the Iron Range, or to other locations in nearby northern Wisconsin.

4. While visiting Duluth, check out the calendar of events for the Twin Ports Horror Society. The group was started by Cory Jezierski on Facebook and has grown to over a thousand members. Besides offering a place for like-minded people to meet up online, the

group meets in person for movie showings, events, and an annual Ghoulish Gala.

5. Duluth is a very art-involved community, so make sure to stop by galleries, glass-blowing shops, theaters, and music venues to experience all the city has to offer. Not your speed? Book a session of Duluth Goat Yoga, which will give you fun, relaxation, and an up-close and personal experience with adorable goats.

OTHER SPOOKY PLACES AROUND THE STATE

Anoka

Anoka, Minnesota, is known as the Halloween Capital of the World. The city's website features a countdown clock to Halloween, which, let's admit it, we ALL love. The city hosts multiple parades, a house decorating contest, and a Gray Ghost Run: a 5K run or a one-mile walk. Why did it all begin? To deter youth from participating in Halloween pranks. The volunteer-run tradition began in 1920 with celebrations supporting local schools and scholarships with their family-friendly events.

 Duluth is the home to the annual Catalyst Content Festival, which allows creatives to submit television show pilots and scripts, pitches, web series, novels, podcasts, and more to be nominated for awards. Established in 2006, the festival's mission is to "make it possible for storytellers to make a living they love from where they love living." We have met so many other artists in the horror genre, and other genres, through Catalyst and have made lifelong friends and connections.

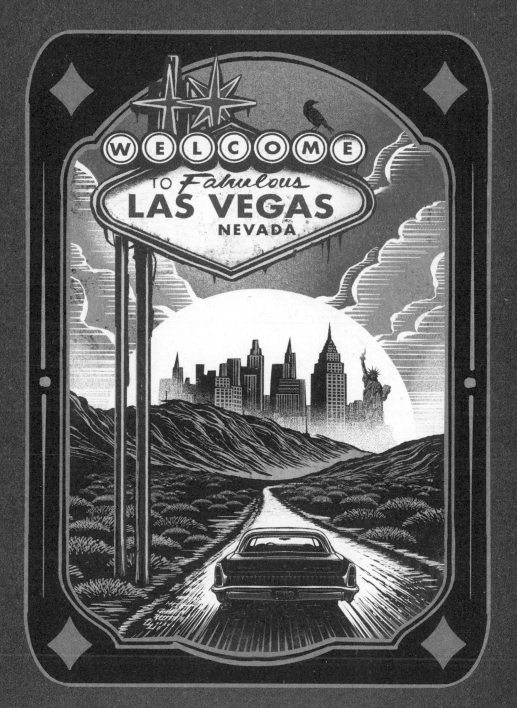

POPULATION: 646,790

SPOOKIEST THING TO HAPPEN HERE

The Luxor, an Egyptian-themed hotel built in 1993, is considered by many to be the most haunted hotel in Las Vegas—ironic because of its relative youth compared to the age of other, older buildings. Yet, the Luxor is home to many tragedies, including suicide and murder.

When it first opened, the hotel provided a free raft ride around the interior that was supposed to be both an attraction as well as help guests get around the enormous pyramid-shaped hotel. The only problem was that multiple guests reported ghost sightings. When the raft went through several dark tunnels, people claimed they were greeted with the apparitions of three workers who had died in the construction of the Luxor. Rumor is, this is the reason the water was drained and the ride was defunct after only three years. In our research, we couldn't find if people actually died during the building of the Luxor, though we found conspiracy theories that these deaths were covered up. Perhaps the ghosts inside those tunnels were actually Egyptian pharaohs angry about the Vegas pyramid? We've stayed at the Luxor several times and haven't experienced any ghostly activity, but we will keep an eye out in the future.

HIDDEN GEM WE DISCOVERED

Sliced Pizza

2129 SOUTH INDUSTRIAL ROAD

Sliced Pizza, located next door to an escape room we attended, was a horror-filled, charming surprise for a bite to eat. Scary movies played on TV screens, horror-themed arcade games lined the walls, and horror decor and collectibles could be found throughout. The charcoal-black pizza crust was unique and delicious as we watched *Better Watch Out* (2016) on the TVs. After we spoke to the owner, we were brought a poster of the movie that was signed by the director and that read, "Get Sliced!" The best part of Sliced Pizza? Life-size *Ghoulies* (1985) figures looming over us as we ate. If you know us, we recommend *Ghoulies III: Ghoulies Go to College* (1985) for the most perfect horror-comedy combination of all time (in our opinion).

 # MOST FAMOUS TRUE CRIME

Sin City is known for myriad crimes, but perhaps the most notorious is the murder of beloved rapper Tupac Shakur in 1996. Hit four times by targeted gunfire in a drive-by shooting, Shakur died six days after the violent attack. The rap community was forever changed by Shakur's death, which resulted in controversy over the true culprit of the crime. It is still officially unsolved, as the main suspect, Orlando Anderson, a member of the South Side Crips, died in 1998. There's an informal shrine to honor the rapper near the Las Vegas Strip, and some advocates are pushing for a formal memorial.

SPOOKY MOVIES AND BOOKS SET HERE

BOOKS

Desperation (1996) by
   Stephen King

The Hunger (2018) by
   Alma Katsu

We Sold Our Souls (2018) by
   Grady Hendrix

MOVIES

Spirits of the Dead (1968)

Tremors (1990)

Fright Night (2011)

 # WHAT TO DO

Vegas Ghosts: Gangsters, Glitz, and Gore Tour

VARIOUS MEETING SITES

We are huge fans of the US Ghost Adventures tours, and their Las Vegas offering did not disappoint. Our guide, Jordan, really knew his stuff. And he and Kelly talked A LOT about musical theater. So, yeah, he was an appreciated new friend in Vegas. Right away we were struck with

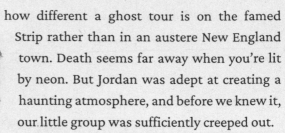

how different a ghost tour is on the famed Strip rather than in an austere New England town. Death seems far away when you're lit by neon. But Jordan was adept at creating a haunting atmosphere, and before we knew it, our little group was sufficiently creeped out.

Nearly every casino we passed had a dark history. Many of the ghost stories included victims of suicide, as the highs and lows of gambling took their emotional toll. In fact, we learned most hotels in the city do not have balconies for this very reason.

Quite a few famous ghosts have been spotted in Vegas, including the mobster Bugsy Siegel, founder of the Flamingo. He is said to linger in the casino, dressed to the nines in his expensive suit. This is particularly haunting, as Siegel didn't live to see his casino fully built.

Area 15: Universal Monsters
3215 SOUTH RANCHO DRIVE

A few weeks after we left Las Vegas, Universal Studios made an exciting announcement for classic horror fans. They are installing a permanent horror experience in Area15, an "immersive playground" that is already home to such awesome fun, like zombie virtual reality and ax throwing. The "Universal Monsters"–themed experience will be a year-round haunted house, honoring cinematic legends Frankenstein's monster, Wolfman, Dracula, the Mummy, and, we certainly hope, the first woman of horror: the Bride of Frankenstein. There is no word when this Las Vegas attraction will open, but we'll be there ASAP. See you in the haunted halls?

Madame Tussauds Wax Museum

3377 SOUTH LAS VEGAS BOULEVARD

New York City isn't the only home to Madame Tussauds—in fact, there are over twenty locations worldwide. But on our tour, Jordan told us that Madame Tussauds is known as the most haunted spot in Las Vegas. Built in the Venetian on the grounds of what was formerly a celeb hangout, Madame Tussauds is home to many reported ghost sightings. Apparently, a few lucky people have even seen the apparition of Elvis Presley (not just an impersonator at a diner)!

There's no denying that a museum full of wax figures feels like the start of a horror movie. Literally. Like *House of Wax* (1953), starring gothic king Vincent Price. That film undoubtedly caused some people to have a lifelong fear of wax statues, their uncanny faces and lifeless eyes are truly frightening. So why not take a stroll at Madame Tussauds? If the celebrity statues don't unnerve you, maybe you'll get lucky and bump into Elvis. Despite our best hopes, he didn't show himself while we were there. *Sigh*.

The Blair Witch Escape Room

2121 SOUTH INDUSTRIAL ROAD

We booked a time to escape the Blair Witch at this Las Vegas escape room, which is next door to Sliced Pizza. Based on the 1999 movie *The Blair Witch Project*, the escape room had us enter as a "search party" investigating a disappearance in the Burkittsville, Maryland, state forest. We won't give away any details, but we had an absolute blast solving

the mysteries in multiple rooms and were highly impressed with the special effects, props, and storytelling. We may have screamed out loud several times (or maybe only Kelly did) but mainly were smiling ear to ear with how much fun we had.

One thing we appreciated about this escape room is that they let us finish the entire journey, even if we didn't solve every puzzle in time. Hints were given and we could move on to the next room. In experiences elsewhere, if time is up, then you're out. We felt like we got our money's worth, and we loved seeing the intricate story and puzzles that were created. The company also has an escape room with a *Saw* (2004) theme; we plan to book it next. If you don't have a party big enough to book the entire space, don't worry! They will pair you with others to help solve the investigations, and you'll make new friends in the process. And don't forget to stop by the gift shop at the end to purchase some memorabilia that will forever commemorate your sleuthing skills.

Twilight Zone Mini Golf

3645 SOUTH LAS VEGAS BOULEVARD

We made the short walk to the Horseshoe Las Vegas, formerly known as Bally's Las Vegas Hotel and Casino, from Caesars Palace. The lower floor of the Horseshoe is a goth geek's dream! In one corner is the Real Bodies exhibit, an authentic display of human anatomy. This is a permanent installation rather than the traveling anatomy show that may have visited your town. Across from this grotesquerie of dead bodies is the Cabinet of Curiosities, a new gothic-themed bar with an attached speakeasy (more on that later) and, finally, our first stop: Twilight Zone Mini Golf!

When Meg moved to the U.S. in the sixth grade, she'd felt out of place, unmoored by the otherness of Minnesota. But then she discovered the Syfy channel, something that wasn't available in Vancouver at the time. Being able to watch shows like *Tales from the Darkside* and *The Twilight Zone* every day was an instant comfort. *The Twilight Zone* has been such an impactful TV show in her life that she even named the fictional town in her novel series Willoughby after the episode "Last Stop at Willoughby." (She also named her vacuum robot Rod Serling after the creator, because, you know...he loved a robot story.)

So, when we arrived for our eleven o'clock tee time, Meg was immediately thrust into a black-and-white swirl of nostalgia and excitement. For just $12.95 you get to inhabit the Twilight Zone: a black-lit golf course adorned with not just art depicting the episodes but also old-fashioned televisions playing clips and a DJ playing oldies. We're not particularly adept at golf, mini or otherwise, so while we had no real competitive spirit, we putted along to be a part of the mesmerizing aesthetic. It was seriously cool, and as we're both *The Twilight Zone* enthusiasts, we spent most of our time pointing out the references all around us. "Look! It's Burgess Meredith's broken glasses!" "Look! It's that lil' creature that tried to crash William Shatner's plane!"

Zak Bagans Haunted Museum

600 EAST CHARLESTON BOULEVARD

The word on Las Vegas Boulevard and beyond was that this museum, now owned by paranormal investigator Zak Bagans, was the place to go for the horror tourism inclined. Our fellow tour attendees on the Gangsters, Glitz, and Gore Tour all agreed the museum was worth a visit. Unfortunately, due to an impending snowstorm back at home, we missed visiting this notorious institution of the macabre. Oh well; another excuse to travel to Vegas again...

As the website for the museum boasts, "The eleven-thousand-square-foot property built in 1938 was originally owned by prominent business-man Cyril S. Through the years, hostile spirits—family members who passed away there and whose energy remains—have been rumored to roam the halls, terrorizing past occupants. Some longtime Las Vegans even claim dark rituals took place in the home's basement during the 1970s."

Through a bit of research, we found that this businessman who built the home, which has now been turned into the museum, was Cyril S. Wengert. We couldn't uncover anything sinister in his background (though his eight-year-old son died in the residence).

General admission to see all the horror memorabilia is about $50, and if you *really* want the chance to encounter a ghost, the nighttime experience with a souvenir flashlight is $200.

Halloween Emporium and Haunted Tea Room

4555 SOUTH FORT APACHE ROAD

Off the Strip lies the Halloween Emporium and Haunted Tea Room. This shop offers spooky decor and Halloween merchandise year-round as well as events like the Mother Knows Best Tea Party for Mother's Day in 2023. The event taught participants how to make their own tea while *Psycho* (1960) played in the background. Each participant was able to bring home their own teacup and saucer. Now that sounds like our kind of tea party. The shop also sells ghost-hunting equipment if you plan to do some while you're in Las Vegas.

Mob Museum

300 STEWART AVENUE

If you're interested in the history of the Mafia, visit the Mob Museum, located in downtown Las Vegas. With interactive experiences and exhibits, the museum hopes "to advance the public's understanding of organized crime and its impact on American society." One hands-on experience you can take part in is the Crime Lab, which "allows you to explore the work of forensic scientists, fingerprint analysts, DNA profilers, and medical examiners who determine how a crime is committed and secure evidence to the case." The museum also features a distillery tour and tasting where you learn about the culture of drinking from the past and the crimes related to it. Plan to spend anywhere from one to three hours exploring the museum or longer if you partake in one of the experiences.

The Neon Museum

770 LAS VEGAS BOULEVARD NORTH

Purchase tickets in advance for the Neon Museum to see some unique signs. According to its website, "founded in 1996, The Neon Museum is a nonprofit organization dedicated to collecting, preserving, studying, and exhibiting iconic Las Vegas signs for educational, historic, arts, and cultural enrichment." You'll be able to spot the "Betelgeuse" sign from *Beetlejuice* (1988) as well as other historic signs from hotels, exhibits, and restaurants. We recommend visiting at night to see everything lit up. Check out their website to find out tour options and to see what special exhibits are currently on display.

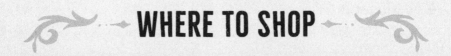

WHERE TO SHOP

Nightmare Toys, Toy Store

1309 SOUTH COMMERCE STREET

If you intend to visit Nightmare Toys, plan to spend some time and money there. Owned by lifelong horror fan Kristy Adams, the store contains everything your goth heart desires, from shoes that spell "REDRUM" when put together (which Kelly purchased) to a *Candyman* figure signed by actor Tony Todd (Meg eyed it longingly). We always appreciate when a horror shop is owned by a true, authentic fan, and you can tell how much love has gone into making Nightmare Toys a destination to hit up while in Las Vegas.

Blaspheme Boutique, Horror Boutique

1750 SOUTH RAINBOW BOULEVARD

There are shops everywhere on the Strip, yet most of them are the typical designer clothes and tourist baubles. If you're seeking a truly unique experience, head off the main Las Vegas drag and check out Blaspheme Boutique. They have witchy clothes, tarot cards, and goth home decor, and they provide astrology and psychic readings. You can also shop their online boutique if you never quite make it out of your casino-hotel or don't have room in your luggage on the way home.

Cash 4 Chaos, Thrift Store
4110 SOUTH MARYLAND PARKWAY

Another must-stop shop is Cash 4 Chaos. This is the perfect place to hunt for thrifted goods that honor your fave punk bands or horror movies. Our favorite finds? A *Demons* (1985) T-shirt we hadn't seen before, a Jack Skellington onesie baby gift for a friend, and a black pullover hoodie with Vampira's picture on it. Perfect for those cool nights and Minnesota winters.

Rockin Bettie, Clothing Store
1302 SOUTH THIRD STREET

For those retro folks looking for a vintage rockabilly vibe, Rockin Bettie, founded by lifelong Vegas resident Amy Ortiz, is your best bet for a polka-dot swing dress or (our favorite) the showstopping Manhattan leopard pencil dress. We'll take ten, thanks! With inclusive sizing, quality items, and limited production, you know you'll be getting an individual look that not everyone else will be sporting.

WHERE TO STAY

Caesars Palace

3570 SOUTH LAS VEGAS BOULEVARD

We stayed at Caesars Palace during our latest trip to Las Vegas and were thrilled with the space and view we received. Established in 1966, Caesars is designed to emulate the Roman Empire and is filled with iconography reflecting Hollywood Roman-period productions. We enjoyed the multitude of restaurants on site, including Vanderpump Lounge, Gordon Ramsay's Pub and Grill, and Cafe Americano. Window-shop at the high-end boutiques located in the Forum, which is the highest-grossing mall in the United States, or people-watch in one of the many casinos on site.

While we had a comfortable stay, not everyone has been so lucky. Some people have reported automatic faucets turning on and off by themselves, and one craps table was said to be haunted. Casino expert Adrian Sireca of Online Casino Gems said, "Caesars Palace is one of the most fun casinos in Vegas, and one of the most sinister. Many gamblers with a penchant for the dark and mysterious have been drawn to it, and I expect that many more will in the future as well." Check out the casino for yourself and play one of the horror-themed slot machines if you're into it. One of our favorite moments was seeing an Elvis impersonator eating breakfast at a twenty-four-hour diner. Hail to the King, baby.

Circus Circus

While we personally haven't stayed at Circus Circus, we have heard how creepy and haunted the property is. While perusing the casino on our latest visit, we felt like we had walked into a horror movie. Children? Clowns? Magic acts happening 24/7? We experienced it all within minutes of exploring. Opened in 1968, Circus Circus contains the largest permanent circus in the world but also has a sinister past. With its multiple murders and deaths by suicide occurring in the hotel, guests have reported seeing wandering spirits, hearing strange noises, and witnessing objects moving on their own. If that wasn't enough to deter us from staying any longer than we did, the large neon clown sign welcoming people in was a bit creepy to us. Yes, we've probably been warped by watching Pennywise too much in the *It* (2017) movies, but we choose to stay elsewhere when visiting Vegas.

The rooms are inexpensive, and the hotel has the only RV park on the Strip where you can book a spot that includes an on-site pool, laundry facilities, and showers. It's important to note that the walkability past Circus Circus may be sketchy, according to locals. Use a rideshare to travel past the property to downtown Vegas or beyond for safety reasons.

 There are plenty of possible road trips you can take through Nevada that will lead you to ghost towns, haunted hotels, and beauties of nature. Be aware that cell phone coverage may not be available everywhere, especially in remote locations. Sounds like the perfect setup for a horror movie.

The Lexi

501 WEST SAHARA AVENUE

If you're looking for a place to stay closer to downtown, try the Lexi, formerly known as the Artisan Hotel Boutique. When you enter the lobby filled with gothic art, you'll know you're in for a treat. No two rooms or suites are alike in this sixty-four-room hotel, so you'll experience your own themed room with artwork to match. On site there's a bar, restaurant, and European pool (which means tops are optional). This property became cannabis friendly in 2023, with an entire floor that features state-of-the-art air filtration systems and a cannabis lounge on the ground floor.

Off the Strip

On one visit to Las Vegas, we rented an Airbnb in a quiet residential neighborhood off the Strip. Renting a home has its advantages and disadvantages. For one, we had our own private pool to swim in and quiet surroundings to get plenty of restful sleep. At the same time, being farther away from the action made us feel less like we were on vacation, especially because we felt the need to grocery shop and cook meals to utilize the gorgeous kitchen in the home. Depending on what kind of trip you're looking for, check out the options for homes or apartments to rent in Las Vegas. It may be the perfect option for you.

Nightmare Café

1307 SOUTH COMMERCE ROAD

Looking for a horror-themed restaurant with a full bar in Las Vegas? Make a reservation at Nightmare Cafe. Located not far from the Nightmare Toys shop and owned by the same woman, the restaurant features fun and clever menu items like Poultrygeist (buttermilk fried chicken), Portrait of a Salad Killer, and Kujo (a bacon-wrapped hotdog). The ambience and decorations are just as you would expect as you find yourself surrounded by murals, decor, and fright flicks playing in the background. The Nightmare Cafe holds biweekly horror trivia and is a casual and fun atmosphere for any horror fan. Order drinks like the Invisible-Man-Hattan, the Bloody Carrie, or the Psycho Sour. Pro-tip: Order the Fang Banger drink, which comes in an IV drip bag. You'll need to recharge after all the shopping next door.

Heart Attack Grill

450 EAST FREMONT STREET

What's scarier than eating food that can potentially increase the chances of giving you a heart attack? Weighing yourself before you go in. It's not a requirement to step on the scale, but customers weighing in over 350 pounds eat for free at the Heart Attack Grill. Located on Fremont Street in Las Vegas, this hospital-themed restaurant includes servers dressed as doctors and nurses taking orders they dub "prescriptions" from customers, or "patients." Each customer is given a hospital gown and wristband before ordering. Anyone who finishes their Triple or Quadruple Bypass Burger is given a ride to their vehicle in a wheelchair. While it may not totally be our jam, we did find the restaurant appropriately horrifying.

The Cabinet of Curiosities

3645 SOUTH LAS VEGAS BOULEVARD

If you feel like solving a mystery while being surrounded by objects from around the world, have a drink at the Cabinet of Curiosities, located in the Horseshoe in Las Vegas. We enjoyed cocktails made by mixologists that were created after the themes in the surrounding exhibits, including the Curious Cosmopolitan and the Pink Stone Egg. We spent time exploring the cabinets filled with all sorts of knickknacks and used QR codes to learn more about their history.

If you see a vintage phone, pick it up to receive the password to the Lock, located next door. This hidden speakeasy requires you to solve some puzzles before entering then answer questions based on your current mood. Your responses will determine the drink that's made just for you. A truly unique and fun experience, The Cabinet of Curiosities can become an entire afternoon or evening of mystery or can be a cozy atmosphere to enjoy a drink or two.

Diablo's Cantina

3400 SOUTH LAS VEGAS BOULEVARD

Any place with a sinister or dark theme immediately gets our attention, and when we saw the sign for this restaurant, we had to stop. With locations in both the Luxor and the Mirage, Diablo's Cantina offers delicious Mexican food with a fun atmosphere. Colorful skeleton murals adorn the walls, and we enjoyed house margaritas, enchiladas, and tacos for dinner.

 # A WOMAN YOU SHOULD KNOW

Virginia Hill

(1916–1966)

While on our US Ghost Adventures tour of the Strip, tour guide Jordan told us the fascinating history behind the legendary Flamingo casino. Apparently, mobster Bugsy Siegel named his casino for his mistress, Virginia Hill, whose cheeks would blush pink when she drank alcohol. This is a charming tale, with some naysayers on the internet, but whether it's true or not, it was a snapshot into the tumultuous love affair between Siegel and Hill.

This was our first time learning of Virginia Hill, who was an intimidating gangster in her own right. After enduring a traumatic childhood, during which she married at age fourteen, Hill moved to Chicago. She worked her way from being a sex worker to a cocktail waitress at Al Capone's hangout to eventually getting involved in money laundering for mobsters like Joe Epstein. At one time considered the "Queen of the Mob," Hill built a successful crime business in LA and Vegas.

She is best known for dating the married Bugsy Siegel, who, like many other men in her life, physically abused her. Suffering from mental health issues, Hill was unfortunately susceptible to men who hurt her. As Jordan told us, according to stories, after receiving a particularly awful beating by Siegel in 1947, Hill stormed out of her Beverly Hills home, and soon after the famous Siegel was gunned down. Just as with the shooting death of Tupac Shakur in Vegas decades later, no one was ever charged with Siegel's murder. He had many enemies, but some believe it was associates of Virginia Hill who took him out on her behest after one too many vicious assaults.

Hill died by suicide in Austria, where she was hiding from the U.S. Government, at age forty-nine. This tragic story stuck with us as we passed the beautiful Vegas institution of the Flamingo. We wondered if someone as clever as Virginia Hill could've lived a better life if she'd been given better, less criminal opportunities. She is one of many people who played too hard in Las Vegas.

 Hoover Dam, standing seventy stories high, is about a forty-minute drive from Las Vegas and was constructed between 1931 and 1936. One hundred and twelve deaths occurred during the building of the dam, and an additional forty-two people died from what was considered pneumonia. Some speculate that it was actually carbon monoxide poisoning. Reports of hauntings include flickering lights, changes in temperature, and the sounds of water dripping even when the source is not apparent.

TRAVEL TIPS

1. Don't forget to check visitlasvegas.com for daily events. There's a good chance there will be pop-ups or shows with gothic flair like the "atomic age comedy" *Zombie Burlesque* at Planet Hollywood.

2. Although much of the Strip in Las Vegas is walkable, we recommend taking a rideshare for certain areas. More from tired feet than from feelings of fear, we called a rideshare after our visit to Circus Circus to bring us the rest of the way to the escape room. Our driver encouraged us not to walk in the area for safety, and we were glad to know this for future visits.

3. The Vegas airport may be the only place we couldn't find vegetarian options. With only a few restaurants to choose from, we were resigned to chips and salsa at the place we chose for lunch and resorted to eating snacks from a gift shop to round out our meal. To enjoy more options, eat before you come to the airport.

4. Las Vegas is in the desert and gets HOT in the summer (we're talking an average high of 107 degrees Fahrenheit in July). Travel smart, hydrate, and wear sunscreen when outside. We goths need to protect our precious tattoos and our sensitive skin! We prefer to visit Vegas in the fall and winter months, like when the January average high is 59, which is a warm respite from our own cold surroundings.

5. While flights to Las Vegas are often affordable from multiple cities, consider a road trip from Los Angeles. While it's still a four-hour drive, you'll experience multiple unique sights along the way, including Seven Magic Mountains, an art installation in the middle of the desert featuring seven brightly colored boulder totems; the World's Largest Chevron Station; and Bonnie and Clyde's Death Car. If you don't feel like stopping, you may spot truly random things like we did, such as a man smoking a cigarette next to a burning trailer and a woman vomiting with her arms over her head. Horror is all around us, friends.

OTHER SPOOKY PLACES AROUND THE STATE

Tonopah

Located between Reno and Las Vegas in the town of Tonopah, Nevada, stands "America's Scariest Motel." The Clown Motel, as its name clearly states, is filled with Clarence David's beloved collection of clowns. Each room features clown art, and guests have reported paranormal activity on the premises.

Massacre Lake

The Massacre Rim Dark Sky Sanctuary in Nevada is one of only fifteen Dark Sky Sanctuaries in the world. One of the most remote and darkest places on earth got its name when settlers on the Oregon Trail mistook stone markers for graves.

Pyramid Lake

North America's oldest known petroglyphs were found near Pyramid Lake in Nevada, dating back to between 10,500 and 14,800 years ago. The area's rich Indigenous history of the Paiute people is documented at the Pyramid Lake Visitor Center.

WELCOME TO

PITTSBURGH

PENNSYLVANIA

POPULATION: 300,431

SPOOKIEST THING TO HAPPEN HERE

Henry Clay Frick, an industrialist in Pittsburgh, was saved from an attempted assassination by the ghost of his daughter, Martha. On July 23, 1892, a man burst into Frick's office with a loaded revolver and a sharpened steel file intending to kill him. The man shot, and according to Frick, the apparition of his deceased daughter temporarily blinded the would-be assassin and caused him to miss, allowing Frick to survive a second shot that grazed him. He did suffer stab wounds from the file but fully gave credit to his daughter for saving him. The Frick Building still stands in downtown Pittsburgh, and some believe you can see the ghost of Martha peering down from a window.

HIDDEN GEM WE DISCOVERED

Jekyl and Hyde

140 SOUTH EIGHTEENTH STREET

Jekyl and Hyde, a Halloween-themed bar in Pittsburgh, is decorated with creepy decor, has jack-o'-lantern trick-or-treat buckets filled with candy on the counter, and features fun, horror-themed cocktails. *Friday the 13th Part 2* (1981) was playing on one of the televisions, and a Michael Myers life-size statue stood behind us, presumably judging our choices. We enjoyed a Jag-O-Lantern, Jekyl and Hyde's signature drink, made with vanilla, orange, and whipped cream–flavored vodka and orange liqueur, as well as one called a Coffin Club, made with lemonade-flavored vodka and triple sec. Owned and operated by women, the bar is a must-see for horror fans, and you can even get your karaoke fix here weekly. Anyone up for singing "Monster Mash" by Bobby Pickett with us?

MOST FAMOUS TRUE CRIME

A passionate love affair is often at the center of the most notorious crimes. This is no different in the heart of steel country. In 1902, Katherine Soffel, the wife of the Allegheny County Jail warden, fell madly in love with convicted murderer Ed Biddle—so madly, in fact, that she helped Biddle and his brother escape her husband's jail.

The Biddle brothers were soon to be executed for their time in the "Chloroform Gang," which, let's be honest, speaks for itself. Despite her lover's poor life choices, Soffel stole firearms for him and accompanied the two escapees in a stolen truck heading north. They were hoping to cross the Canadian border, but fate intervened. Allegheny and Butler County police killed the Biddles in a shootout. Katherine Soffel lived through the escape. She did time for her crimes in her husband's jail, then opened up her own seamstress shop shortly before her death. A woman falling in love with a criminal is a tragic story as old as time. Maybe one day it'll work out?

SPOOKY MOVIES AND BOOKS SET HERE

BOOKS

Imaginary Friend (2019) by
  Stephen Chbosky
The Corpse Queen (2021) by
  Heather M. Herman

MOVIES

Night of the Living Dead (1968)
The Visit (2015)
Scary Stories to Tell in the Dark
  (2019)

 The Kecksburg UFO incident, which took place in 1965, is part of local lore in Pittsburgh. On December 9 of that year, a fireball was seen in the sky over six U.S. states, and in the village of Kecksburg, Pennsylvania, several people reported hearing a thump, seeing wisps of blue smoke, and feeling vibrations during the incident. Although the government claims to have never recovered anything at the scene, locals and out-of-towners alike wonder if there's more to the story. National media outlets and some filmmakers have followed the occurrence and suggested possible explanations for the events, including the object being a Soviet satellite, a meteor, or even a Nazi UFO. Kecksburg holds an annual UFO Festival, which benefits the local fire department. Visit their website for merch and information.

Allegheny Cemetery

4734 BUTLER STREET

Incorporated in 1844, the Allegheny Cemetery is located on Butler Street in Pittsburgh and is home to numerous graves ranging from impressive mausoleums to humble headstones for unknown soldiers. As we were dropped off at the gates of the cemetery, we were impressed with the historic buildings on the premises. The cemetery's website notes that the grounds offer a pleasant place to walk, and we witnessed many parties taking part in it. The wide walkways, pristine grounds, and historical graves were a calming and poignant place to explore for an afternoon. Of note, we sought out a grave that was mentioned to us, one that featured the film *Jaws* (1975) on its headstone. In a distinctive shape of a great white's nose, the stone is etched with the fearsome teeth of the shark, echoing the famous *Jaws* poster. We had heard a couple different versions of why the headstone existed. One was that it commemorates a crew member who worked on the film and wanted to honor the movie's legacy. The true story, though, reveals that it was a super fan of the franchise who died at the age of fifty-one. A Korean War veteran, Lester C. Madden was a fan of the films and chose this as his gravestone. Seeing it in person, we pondered what shape and form our future headstones will be. Regardless, we salute Mr. Madden as a trendsetter for following his passion and love of the horror genre.

As we continued to tour the cemetery, numerous geese honked and pecked at the ground while we passed. Our GPS and phone service were spotty while we navigated our way out of the cemetery, and we declared it felt like "the beginning of a horror movie." Eventually we made our way out and on to our next destination. We also both declared that if we lived in the Lawrenceville area of Pittsburgh, we would walk the cemetery daily.

Monroeville Mall

200 MALL CIRCLE DRIVE, MONROEVILLE

Meg was about ten years old, a lil' horror fan in training, when she stumbled across a VHS copy of *Dawn of the Dead* (1978) at her local Blockbuster. She was instantly mesmerized by George A. Romero's classic, and it became a touchstone of her childhood. Meg went by Blockbuster for many weeks afterward, using her allowance to rent the movie over and over again. *Dawn of the Dead* was a hypnotizing cocktail of vibrant color, matter-of-fact violence, and best of all, it took place in the Mecca of all preteen happiness, a mall. This film and Romero's other works have left a profound mark on what we both strive for today in horror: fun, diverse, female-driven horror stories that have something to say. *Dawn of the Dead* made metaphorical use of its mall setting, making a statement about the slavish nature in which we humans mindlessly shop for things we don't need, you know, just like how zombies consume brains.

Pittsburgh native George A. Romero is a hometown hero, highly respected for his cerebral approach to horror filmmaking. The University of Pittsburgh has established the George A. Romero Foundation, whose website we encourage you to check out. Not only do they have an impressive archive on site at the university, but they also do a number of online events each year, which we both have been lucky enough to attend. These have included a tour of some of the most impressive and unique Romero artifacts, like hand-drawn scene sketches, as well as a showing of the previously unreleased short film *Jacaranda Joe*.

A visit to Monroeville Mall in the close-by suburb of Monroeville was a peek into zombie history. From the outside it looks like any other mall in America, flanked by a Barnes & Noble and a JCPenney. We walked into the wing known as Romero Court, where upstairs there is a hall dedicated to the filming of *Dawn of the Dead*. Posters show screenshots, as well as a certificate from the *Guinness Book of Records* boasting that in 2006 the biggest gathering of people dressed as zombies was recorded at Monroeville Mall. (If you're curious, it was 894.) And if you want to get into this walking-dead action, plan a trip to the mall when there is an official Living Dead weekend. These horror-packed events include celebrity visits from the film's actors, as well as panels, parties, and horror memorabilia vendors.

While you stroll along the mall you'll find the Living Dead Museum, both a horror gift shop and a small collection of film history. As Bruce Campbell's number one fan, Kelly was particularly happy with the Evil Dead artifacts, as well as their impressive selection of Campbell T-shirts.

And don't forget to stop by the arcade in Monroeville Mall for ZombieBurgh Lazer Tag, where you can pretend you're in the movie and shoot at the undead!

A lot has changed since the filming of *Dawn of the Dead* in the late 1970s. The iconic fountain is gone, as is the skating rink, and, thankfully, no flesh-eating zombies were milling about, though we could still feel the manic energy of one of our favorite movies.

Downstairs in Romero Court, you will find a bust of the filmmaker, who passed away in 2017. Beneath his visage is a short biography touting him as an "American visionary." We couldn't agree more! At the bottom is a quote from Romero: "The neighbors are scary enough when they're not dead."

Gypsy Parlor Tattoo

4601 PENN AVENUE

Why not get some new ink in Steel City? Our Pittsburgh friend Stephanie told us that the all-female Gypsy Parlor Tattoo is the place to go. And if we hadn't just gotten our matching ghosties in St. Augustine, we'd have been all over it. We need a little time to heal before our next needle sesh!

Mayview Mental Hospital, built in the late 1800s and first known as the Marshalsea Poor House, housed those considered insane, which included single mothers up until the 1940s. Like many other state-run hospitals, Mayview closed its doors in 2008, and its occupants were either moved to other facilities for care or were released. The building and land were purchased and eventually demolished in 2016.

Coop De Ville

2305 SMALLMAN STREET

We had to check out the Strip District of Pittsburgh after quite a few locals suggested we'd like the food and shops. On weekends the Strip is known to host international food markets. We were there on a cold Tuesday evening, an understandably quiet time to wander along the revitalized buildings. Our Pittsburgh-native friend told us that Coop De Ville, a fast-casual fried chicken joint, held a nice little surprise of horror inside.

We weren't disappointed when we tripped into a horror pinball haven. Attack from Mars! The Shadow! There was also our all-time favorite: the Addams Family pinball that Meg had spent much of the '90s trying to defeat in the darkened arcade of an Embassy Suites.

Thirty years later and she still hasn't exactly schooled that pinball yet... We guess we'll have to come back to Pittsburgh and try again.

RandyLand

1501 ARCH STREET

We like to ask locals (rideshare drivers, servers, gravediggers) about the quirkiest places to visit. One driver, Paul Spilsbury, is a self-proclaimed man from Mars—Mars, Pennsylvania, that is. According to Paul and other Pittsburghians, RandyLand was the unanimous winner.

A free attraction on the city's north side, visiting RandyLand is what we imagine it must be like to walk into the brain of its creator, Randy Gilson. In the mid-'90s, Gilson began decorating his home and surrounding lawn with eclectic treasures others had thrown away. Full of color, RandyLand is a monument to fun and positivity. Amid the nostalgic collection of toys, RandyLand is home to the most international welcome signs (all painted by Gilson), as well as a plethora of kind-worded aphorisms to remind you to be well. We're pretty confident even the most somber of goths would smile here, imbued with sparkly rainbows in RandyLand. From pillars adorned with forgotten My Little Ponies to Gilson's hand-painted biography, there is an undeniable charm that, black-hearted as we may appear, we are not immune to. Although it was a breezy cold day in Pittsburgh, we were instantly warmed by the character of RandyLand.

Andy Warhol Museum

117 SANDUSKY STREET

The Andy Warhol Museum, featuring rotating exhibits, is located in the heart of Pittsburgh's Pop District and was established in 1994. Warhol was born and raised in the city and was the leading figure in visual art known as "pop art." The museum holds the largest collection of Warhol's work and is the largest single-artist museum in North America.

The museum's vision is to be "a global destination for scholarship and learning about Warhol's life, art, and relevance to contemporary culture." Kelly has to admit that she was excited to see the Campbell's-themed art most of all because her son is named Campbell, after Bruce Campbell, the horror actor. She was definitely impressed with the theme, but overall, the museum does not disappoint, as it's filled with a variety of types of art that you can immerse yourself in. The museum's art collection includes "nine hundred paintings; approximately one hundred sculptures; nearly two thousand works on paper; more than one thousand published and unique prints; four thousand photographs; sixty feature films; two hundred Screen Tests; and more than four thousand videos. The collection also features Warhol wallpaper and books." If you're in town longer, check out their schedule of events for all ages, including gallery talks, art workshops, and other series that teach, inspire, and help you create.

WHERE TO STAY

The Omni William Penn

530 WILLIAM PENN PLACE

The Omni William Penn, built during World War I, was founded by Henry Clay Frick (remember him from earlier?), who had the hotel's facade designed using the principles of Beaux Arts architecture. The hotel underwent a renovation in the 1950s that made the William Penn the second-tallest structure of its kind in the world.

The grand lobby greets guests with antique furniture, beautiful chandeliers, and a welcoming atmosphere. There are touches of history throughout the hotel, including a mail chute that descends from the top floors of the hotel, a shoeshine station, and, just off the lobby, a gallery of photos and memorabilia from the hotel's past.

Our comfortable room overlooked downtown Pittsburgh, and we kept our eyes and ears open for any ghostly activity. One story from the William Penn includes guests hearing a panda bear bleating. How could this be? Well, in 1947, fashion designer and writer Ruth Harkness died at the hotel. She had brought a panda from China back to the United States a decade earlier and named her Su Lin. She bottle-fed it formula on the plane while she held it in her arms. The panda ended up at the Brookfield Zoo in Chicago, but some believe the bear is still looking for the woman who brought her to America all those years ago.

Other guests have reported hearing voices and strange sounds, and feeling cold breezes coming from the top two floors, which are closed off to guests. In 1922 a traveling salesman died by suicide on either the twenty-second or twenty-third floor, both of which are currently being used for storage. This may explain the eerie disturbances guests experience.

We appreciated the convenience of the location of the hotel, the on-site restaurants and bars, and the excellent customer service we received during our stay. We'll definitely be back to the Omni William Penn, and we'll keep searching for Su Lin, the ghost panda.

Renaissance Pittsburgh Hotel

107 SIXTH STREET

Another infamous hotel in Pittsburgh known for being haunted is the Renaissance Hotel. Built in 1906, the Fulton Building, now the Renaissance Pittsburgh Hotel, was once used as a veterans' hospital, a night court, a trade school, and even a dance club. The building became a hotel in 2001, and guests and employees have reported strange occurrences, including seeing a female ghost.

According to the *Visit Pittsburgh* website, "One guest saw a photo of famous painter Mary Cassatt hanging in the hotel and said that was the woman they had seen." The prolific artist was born in Allegheny City, now part of Pittsburgh, in 1844 and passed away in France in 1926. She was known for her perceptive depictions of women and children in her work and her purposeful omission of men. She wrote, "Women should be someone not something," and her legacy will live on for generations. As *New York Times* writer Cotter Holland stated, "Politically, her thinking was progressive, in a moderate, class-bound way. She was witty, intelligent, with no obvious signs of disruptive personal quirks. She has even come to feel like a contemporary, which means like a desirable dinner partner: urbane, unsentimental, reticent without being shy." This is one ghost we wouldn't mind running into.

WHERE TO EAT

Roland's Seafood Grill

1904 PENN AVENUE

Located in the Strip District, Roland's Seafood Grill caught our attention with its lobster logo, which reminded us of a "lobstrosity" from Stephen King's *Dark Tower* series and, of course, the name, which is the same as that of the main character from the books. The restaurant began in the early 1940s when Roland Chelini opened his first location, called the Rail Restaurant. As we discovered in our research of the area, many places opened at 2:00 a.m. to feed the workers in the city who were employed as steelworkers, truck drivers, and produce workers. The current location opened in 1992 and has undergone several changes, including new menus, new seating, and new owners. We enjoyed drinks and a seafood dinner in the multilevel restaurant.

Ritual House

524 WILLIAM PENN PLACE

Opened in early 2023, Ritual House is just steps away from the Omni William Penn. Formerly the Union Trust Building, built by Henry Clay Frick, a recurring figure in this chapter, the restaurant is an absolutely stunning space to walk into. With chairs hanging from the ceiling in the entryway to custom-made furniture from Turkey, every detail of our dining experience was immaculate. The owners promise Pittsburgh favorites to be reimagined, and we were pleasantly surprised by the service, decor, and overall feeling of the establishment.

Black Forge Coffee

1206 ARLINGTON AVENUE

We had the chance to meet up with local Pittsburgh professor and author Stephanie Wytovich (*Writing Poetry in the Dark,* 2022) for some much-appreciated caffeine and conversation at Black Forge Coffee. The female-owned heavy metal—themed establishment was the perfect setting for three horror authors to meet up, talk about all things spooky, and learn more about the wonderful city of Pittsburgh.

Try a hot or cold version of the Gravedancer, a chai latte with vanilla and violet syrups and nutmeg, or a drink called the Hellhound, an espresso with dark chocolate, chili, cinnamon, and cream served over ice. The space is the perfect place to get some work done, visit with friends, or attend an event like Heavy Metal Karaoke or Yoga from the Crypt.

It was so lovely to see how passionate Stephanie is about her city. This chapter wouldn't exist without her help and enthusiasm! Read more about her in "A Woman You Should Know".

The Church Brew Works

3525 LIBERTY AVENUE

The Church Brew Works is located in the former St. John the Baptist church. In what was originally the Lawrenceville area, the brewery features a rotating list of craft beers, a full menu, and a beautiful large space to work, celebrate, or enjoy some drinks. We appreciate former churches and other spaces being turned into viable arts and entertainment venues, and the Church Brew Works is an excellent example of how to repurpose an amazing structure, especially with its original stained-glass art intact.

The Abbey

4635 BUTLER STREET

The Abbey, located within steps of the Allegheny Cemetery, is a former foundry turned funeral home turned coffeehouse, restaurant, and bar. The space features original ceilings, exposed-brick walls, and original wrought iron elevator door panels from Pittsburgh's Jenkin's Arcade. Our server pointed out the chandelier hanging over the coffeehouse and explained that it is a reclaimed rose window from Our Lady Help of Christian Church, which was located in Pittsburgh's Larimer neighborhood. It's also used as the Abbey's logo and is a stunning addition to the space. We sat in a small library area and soaked up the ambience while sipping our coffee and eyeing the homemade pastries. We made sure to also visit the Vesper Room in the establishment, which is filled with reclaimed oak paneling and stained-glass windows from the demolished Mary S. Brown Methodist Church, which was once in the area. It's decorated with vintage signs and photos, and we had a fun time looking at all the decor.

While we enjoyed drinks and dinner, we learned about Pittsburgh's signature sandwich, the Primanti, which had also been recommended to us by numerous locals. The sandwich includes a grilled meat of your choice between two pieces of Italian bread with melted provolone, vinegar-based coleslaw, tomatoes, and french fries. The sandwich was born in the Strip District in Pittsburgh when workers discovered it was easier to eat their meal all at once in the form of a sandwich instead of stopping to eat at a table with a knife and fork. The sandwich could also be eaten with only one hand, which made it convenient for truck drivers in the area.

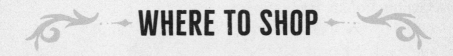

WHERE TO SHOP

The Weeping Glass, Horror Shop

746 EAST WARRINGTON AVENUE

If the store description of "oddness and ephemera" doesn't get you, then we're hoping "sadness and melancholia" will hook you into checking out the Weeping Glass on East Warrington Avenue. If you're a tea goth, there is a skull stirring spoon for your teacup marked "POISON," which you can fill with the Weeping Glass's own loose-leaf varieties with proper names like the Bell Witch and Amityville.

Or maybe you're more of a witchy goth? The Weeping Glass has you covered with a lavender smoke wand, or perhaps you'd fancy a pocket herbal guide? If you're a big spender, then you'll have no problem finding a reason to reach into your black studded wallet. Among other body parts, there's an authentic "geriatric skull" for $1,800.

The Copacetic Comics Company, Comic Shop

3138 DOBSON STREET

Located in a building with a coffee shop and a record store, Copacetic Comics is calling your name. It's stuffed with comics, graphic novels (Meg wanted all of them, but her luggage was overflowing), DVDs, and books. This comic shop and its neighbors are a fun way to spend the afternoon. Copacetic Comics has a strong sense of local pride. They are a small company dedicated to comics above all else, and well, we think that's pretty cool.

Posman Books, Bookstore

1637 SMALLMAN STREET

If you're in the Strip District, pop into Posman Books. Your nostrils will thank you, as OddFellows Ice Cream shares the space, and yep, it smells like sugary heaven. We were impressed with both their nonfiction selection and their robust horror section. Kelly bought a few stickers, and Meg whined about not having any space for books.

Death & Eternity Clothing Co., Clothing

200 MALL CIRCLE DRIVE, MONROEVILLE

While at Monroeville Mall, seeking out all things George Romero, we stumbled upon a shop filled with horror merch that immediately drew us in. We were greeted at Death & Eternity Clothing Co. by friendly staff and started fawning over the Chucky T-shirts, skeleton illustrations, and other horror-themed items all within reach. Because of our limited suitcase space, we each settled on matching tank tops featuring skeletons and the store's logo on the tag. The Black-owned business hopes to be the next Hot Topic and is proud of its inclusive hiring practices. We felt so welcomed and seen in the store, and recommend everyone stop by and pick up some horror merch from Von and his employees.

 Necromancer Brewing in Pittsburgh features an aesthetic for its beer cans that every horror fan will appreciate. With black cans adorned with skulls, skeletons, and other Lovecraftesque creatures, Necromancer features nights like drag bingo, trivia, and a night known as Queer Beer Club.

A WOMAN YOU SHOULD KNOW

Stephanie Wytovich

As we mentioned in "Where to Eat", we had the great pleasure of meeting Stephanie while in Pittsburgh. Raised in rural Pennsylvania, she now calls Pittsburgh home. Wytovich is a force in the horror community, not only in Pittsburgh but globally. We met with her shortly after her most recent Bram Stoker Award nomination for Superior Achievement in Non-Fiction for *Writing Poetry in the Dark* (2022), a collection of essays on inspiration for writing horror poetry. She's been nominated several times in the past for her novels and poetry collections, including a win for her collection *Brothel* in 2017. We were not surprised to find her busily working when we sat down at the table, jotting notes as she read through Shirley Jackson's *We Have Always Lived in the Castle* (1962) in preparation of her next project, *On the Subject of Blackberries*, a poetry collection inspired by the novel. To say Meg is salivating for that book to come out is an understatement. Not only is Wytovich a prolific author and editor, she's also a professor at Point Park University, where she teaches everything from the art of the short story to witch literature. Oh, and she's a mom, too, as well as a champion of other horror creators, and just a really cool lady. In other words, she's our horror-lit-hero witch. Make sure to follow Stephanie Wytovich @SWytovich on Instagram and X, and also check out her blog *Join Me in the Madhouse*.

TRAVEL TIPS

1. Make sure to double-check the open times of your Pittsburgh destinations. Many are closed Mondays and Tuesdays, especially in the slower winter months.

2. If you're driving into Pittsburgh from the airport, watch for the spectacular view as you emerge from the Fort Pitt Tunnel. Our rideshare driver counted down from ten to one, and we were thrilled at the nighttime view of the city.

3. Check local sports schedules (or Taylor Swift concerts) to plan for available hotel rooms and traffic flow. The city is full of concertgoers and sports fans numerous weekends out of the year, and the abundance of travelers can be daunting.

4. If you're looking for an alternative to renting a car or calling a rideshare to travel to Monroeville, you can take a forty-minute Amtrak train (2023 price $8.25) and read a book along the way.

5. To find a number of choices in one spot for your group to eat, stop by the Federal Galley food hall. It features four unique restaurants, a full-service bar, and plenty of local brews to choose from.

OTHER SPOOKY PLACES AROUND THE STATE

Road Trip

There are plenty of haunted and horror-filled places to visit in Pennsylvania, including the Cathedral of Learning in Pittsburgh, the Farnsworth House Inn in Gettysburg, and the Eastern State Penitentiary in Fairmount. If you're able to take a road trip throughout the state, you won't be disappointed.

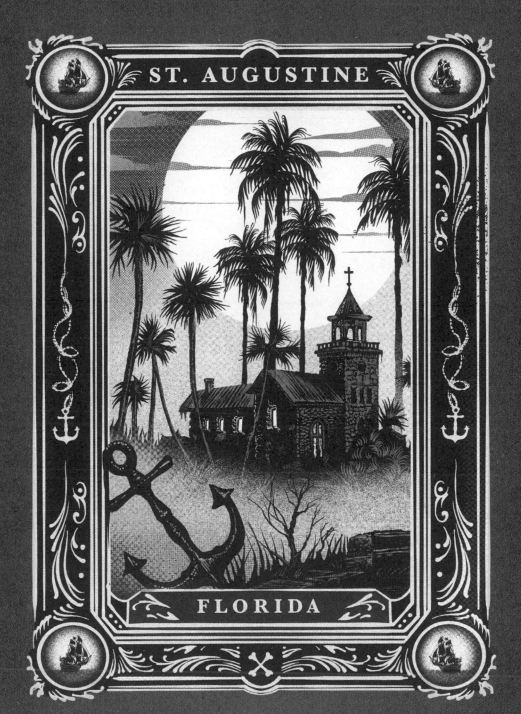

POPULATION: 14,581

SPOOKIEST THING TO HAPPEN HERE

During the construction of the St. Augustine Lighthouse in 1873, five children were playing on a railcar. The brakes on the railcar broke, throwing the children into the sea. Two survived, and it's believed that the three others haunt the lighthouse. As children, the spirits are said to be playful, and visitors have reported hearing giggling, having their shoelaces tied to a staircase, and the sense that the children are playing hide-and-seek.

HIDDEN GEM WE DISCOVERED

Second Read Books

51D CORDOVA STREET

We stumbled across this tiny bookshop thanks to the awesome walkability of St. Augustine. There is so much to explore on foot. What it lacks in size Second Read Books makes up for in their commitment to highlighting and selling local authors. Many of the locally written books focus on the creepy history of St. Augustine, which, yep, is definitely our brand. Also, because the books are used, you're saving the environment *and* saving money. We consider that carte blanche to buy as many books as you want.

 # MOST FAMOUS TRUE CRIME

Athalia Ponsell Lindsley, a model, dancer, and television personality, was murdered in front of her home in St. Augustine in 1974. She was struck nine times with a machete. Her neighbor, who she'd previously had a dispute with, was arrested and brought to trial but was acquitted. Later that same year another neighbor, Frances Bemis, was also found dead. Both murders were never solved.

SPOOKY MOVIES AND BOOKS SET HERE

BOOKS

Ghost Story (1979) by
   Peter Straub
The Between (1995) by
   Tananarive Due
Darkly Dreaming Dexter (2004)
   by Jeff Lindsay

MOVIES

Creature from the Black Lagoon
   (1954)
Day of the Dead (1985)
Crawl (2019)

 # WHAT TO DO

Ghosts & Gravestones Tour

VARIOUS MEETING SITES

We've had the pleasure of taking many ghost tours across this great, spooky country of ours. The Ghosts & Gravestone Tour might just be our favorite. It's tough for the others to compete with, considering it is on an open-air trolley, chock-full of surprises.

We started at a rather typical-looking visitor center. There was some nice ghostie merch we perused before we were asked to line up at a creepy-looking door. Much to our delight, the room we were ushered into was a museum of death. We immediately started taking pics, as it was covered wall to wall with all the macabre baubles we love, like an authentic Victorian traveling mortuary table, death masks, a first-iteration Ouija board, and a dybbuk box, which in Jewish folklore is a cabinet or chest believed to be inhabited by a restless evil spirit. If the dybbuk box is opened, the spirit will obviously wreak havoc. The one who opens the dybbuk box is the person who will be afflicted by the spirit. So, yeah, thankfully there was glass between us and the box, so we didn't have to consider unleashing hell. Because we definitely would've thought about it.

There was a brief talk by our tour guide, Mimi, who is also a high school history teacher. She then had us help open a secret door to the trolley. It was one of those classic bookshelves with the hidden book that's really a lever. Meg swears she's going to have one of those in her house one day. Already charmed by the tour, we loaded up with the other tourists onto the old-timey trolley with bench seats. Mimi was dressed in a Spanish dress from the era of Castillo de San Marcos, the Spanish fort built in St. Augustine starting in 1672. She spoke into a mic from her seat up front. (Our driver was in vintage striped prison garb.) A lifelong resident, Mimi is passionate about the history of her city. She knows just about everything, pointing out local knowledge at every turn.

Our first stop was the Old St Augustine Cemetery. Because of its historical significance we weren't able to step inside the graveyard, but there was a viewing spot where we were told to stand. Mimi shared stories of the people buried there, some under humble stones, others in marble mausoleums surrounded by wrought iron fences with Gothic finials. The most famous dead resident, Mimi said, is six-year-old James, who had climbed one of the cemetery's trees and fallen to his death. A stone was erected where he died. Later, we drove by the corner of the cemetery with the tree and the tragic marker. Little James is known to haunt the tree, appearing in the moonlight to giggle and play.

From the cemetery we walked over to the Potter's Wax Museum. As part of our tour, we were able to go into one of the attraction's rooms. At first, we thought it was just going to be a quick look around. Little did we know one of the "wax figures" would come to life. He successfully scared the crap out of us! Dressed in classic executioner gear, the actor taught us about a famous local pirate, Andrew Ranson. Hilariously using one of our fellow tourists as a proxy for Ranson, the executioner demonstrated how in 1684 the execution of the pirate by garrote (a rope used for strangulation, often affixed with a bar for grip) was botched and Ranson was therefore allowed to live. This decision, of course, was met with great controversy. Ranson went on to be an integral part in the construction of the Castillo San de Marcos thanks to the breaking of the executioner's rope.

This theatrical rendering of history made it all the more fun and memorable. So, we were obviously thrilled when we got to the Old Jail Museum, only to be greeted by the same brand of spooky history. Walking into the jail, constructed in the 1890s, at night was creepy enough, but we were honestly concerned when an "inmate" appeared and locked us up behind steel bars.

The Old Jail was built by the same company as Alcatraz, which isn't hard to believe when you see the fortified inside. It's the sort of soul-less place where criminals become even more hardened and hopeless. We were particularly chilled by the women's part of the jail, where the women were made to do the cooking. Even in jail these women couldn't find freedom from washing dishes.

After our brush with fate in the locked cell, this "inmate" was kind enough to show us the gallows out back. This was a replica in the exact spot where it was in the early twentieth century. He told us how the inmates were made to construct their own gallows, which were torn down after their hanging so the next one could be made. Now that's torture. Kind of like digging your own grave. It was a beautiful night in

St. Augustine as we listened about the fate of these men. The moon shone down on a raccoon that had climbed the tree beside the gallows and looked down at our tour group with a rascally grin. It made me wonder for a moment if that raccoon was really the ghost of an old-timey bandit who had been hanged on that very spot. Or maybe he was just a critter hoping we'd drop crackers from our fanny packs.

We left the jail and continued our tour.

There are many beautiful Spanish churches in St. Augustine, their impressive stained glass glittering in the Florida sun. At night they can give off a more sinister vibe flanked by ancient gravestones. Mimi shared many eerie stories revolving around the city's churches, our favorite being the strange story of the exploding bishop.

In the late nineteenth century, a funeral was held for Bishop Verot, the first Roman Catholic bishop in St. Augustine: "The Florida heat in the middle of June was scorching, and to keep the bishop's body lying in state long enough for mourners to visit, a pit was made in the ground, lined with sawdust and ice, and the bishop's body inserted. An expensive iron, face-plated casket was the only option for this well-known, beloved, and studious man; only the best would be afforded to him for all of his work in Florida and beyond. But imagine for a moment what happens to a dead body subjected to intense heat over a period of three days, sort of like bread dough left in the sun for the yeast to rise. Now imagine, for a moment, putting that mound of bread dough inside an iron oven that's been sealed shut with no expanse for air and excessive temperatures."

Well, you guessed it: during the funeral the iron casket exploded, covering the mourners in the body parts of the bishop. Oops. The pieces of Bishop Verot were interred in the Tolomato Cemetery. In the 1970s he was exhumed in order to verify this bizarre legend. Not only was he, indeed, in pieces, but several were missing. Perhaps they'd been unexpectedly carried home on the clothes of a few traumatized funeral goers?

There were many more twisted tales on the tour. We hope you book your own ticket for the trolley...and can hopefully figure out a way to escape the jail cell.

Castillo de San Marcos
11 SOUTH CASTILLO DRIVE

St. Augustine, purported to be the oldest city in the United States, was settled in 1565. The town features multiple historic buildings, including the oldest wooden schoolhouse in the U.S. and the Castillo de San Marcos, the oldest masonry fort in the U.S. With the city being established so long ago with so much rich history, we were fascinated to learn about the ghost stories that pervade the city. As we learned on our Ghosts & Gravestones Tour, there are some legends of people who were wronged and still haunt the fort. Osceola, a Seminole leader, was imprisoned at Castillo de San Marcos along with two hundred others from his tribe. After his death the doctor "attending" to him decapitated him and kept his head in a jar for display in his drugstore. According to Ghost City Tours, "Visitors often report seeing unexplained shadows walking in the fort, and some claim to have witnessed a headless apparition. Other phenomena include unexpected drops in temperature, sudden chills, and the sound of disembodied voices. These strange sightings have been attributed to the chief, but it could likely be any one of the Native Americans who took their last breath in the prison." Another pair of ghosts that haunt the fort are a couple, Dolores Garcia and Manuel Abela.

After Garcia's husband discovered the couple's affair, he chained them to a wall in the fort, walled over them, and left them to starve. He claimed his wife had left and Abela was on a special mission in Cuba. What gave away their affair? Perfume. Garcia's husband smelled his wife's signature scent on Abela and uncovered their secret affair. Visitors to the fort claim they can sometimes catch a sweet, flowery scent lingering in the air.

The fort is a must-see in St. Augustine. For only fifteen bucks, you get a pass to walk in the fort and on the grounds for a week. Its ancient masonry evokes the castles of Europe. It gave me goose bumps as it was cool and claustrophobic inside, the memories of those who'd built the walls lingering. With its haunted history, you'll be looking over your shoulder as you tour the shadowed corridors. One bummer? The fort is not open at night, so you'll have to hope for ghosts in the daylight.

The Medieval Torture Museum

100 ST. GEORGE STREET

The Medieval Torture Museum in St. Augustine is the largest historical museum in the United States, with over one hundred implements and devices on display. Not for the faint of heart, this museum shows, in gruesome detail, torture and execution scenes. Guests can also listen to an audio tour that tells the stories of people tortured by the devices and the gory details of how each worked. A ghost-hunting app also allows guests to look for ghosts while touring the museum, and they are warned to "keep an eye out for the most terrifying apparition of them all: the ghost of Thomas the Executioner!"

Potter's Wax Museum

31 ORANGE STREET

Potter's Wax Museum can be found in the oldest pharmacy in the United States and also is the oldest wax museum, featuring one hundred and fifty figures with a section devoted to our beloved horror movies. The Ghosts and Gravestones tour offers an after-hours tour called Potter's Wax Chamber of Horrors, which we highly recommend. Being in a wax museum reminds us of one of our favorite Vincent Price movies, *House of Wax* (1953) in which a wax sculptor (Price) uses human corpses under his wax figures. Every set of eyes we looked into, we could almost feel them staring back! Also, having watched too many horror movies, we often felt as if one of the figures would come to life jump-scare style. They didn't on our visit, but you must go and experience this fun museum for yourself.

Fountain of Youth Archaeological Park

11 MAGNOLIA AVENUE

We walked to the Fountain of Youth Archaeological Park and learned much about the area's history. The site is home to an estimated four thousand burials of Timucuan people, who occupied the region since 2,500 BCE. Thankfully, the remains that were discovered were interred in 1991, and exhibits demonstrate the history of the people. We drank from the Fountain of Youth (we'll keep you posted on results), which is considered the oldest attraction in Florida. Guest books date back to 1868, with tourists and school groups keeping the park busy.

Electric Chair Tattoo

701 A1A BEACH BOULEVARD

After such a wonderfully gothic trip to St. Augustine, we wanted a special souvenir to remember our trip by. We did some research for the best tattoo shop in the city and found Electric Chair. With a name like that, how could we resist? We texted the shop that we wanted matching ghosts, and they were able to get us in the next day. Unfortunately, we didn't realize there are three locations of Electric Chair near the beach, a few miles apart, and we got dropped off at the wrong one. Thankfully the employees at the shop were endlessly patient and kind. One of them even fixed Meg's broken phone charger before a long flight, so they basically saved her life.

Our artist, Matt, was super professional. After he found out about our writing this book, he chatted with us about horror books as he gave us adorable ghost tats, right next to our other matching ones; we each have a Grady sister from *The Shining* (1980) on our opposite shoulders. That way they can "hold hands" when we stand next to each other. We totally encourage bestie tattoos like ours, as well as vacation tats. We love to look down at our cartoony ghosts and remember the hot sun and creepy nights of St. Augustine.

St. George Inn

4 ST. GEORGE STREET

We stayed at this lovely historic inn right in the middle of St. Augustine's shopping and tourist district. The St. George Inn is known to be haunted, with rooms 11 and 14 having the most reported activity. The hotel doesn't play up this history, and an employee said she'd never heard of any paranormal activity.

The courtyard of the inn was built over one of the oldest burial grounds in the city, and it's located across the street from a cemetery. People have reported seeing the ghost of a nine-year-old girl, Elizabeth, who died from typhoid fever in the 1800s, standing at the gates of this cemetery.

You won't have trouble finding areas of gothic interest, even right out your window. While sometimes it's nice to stay in hotels of quiet reflection, the St. George Inn is in the action. As soon as you step down from your room to the outdoor courtyard, there are live music, tourists drinking at the attached wine bar, and, thankfully for us, lots of cute dogs passing through. We enjoyed sitting next to the inn's fountain and taking in the Florida sunshine before going to search for darker fare. Kelly found a penny on the ground, so we both made a wish and tossed it in. We won't reveal our wishes, but we will tell you that within *minutes* we received an email making them true.

One night Meg will admit that she was disturbed by something as we slept at the St. George Inn. She woke to footsteps in our room. Naturally she thought it was Kelly getting up to pee. Nope. Meg turned, certain Kelly was up and moving, but she was sound asleep in her bed. Meg's seen enough movies about places built over burial grounds to know it was best to slink down under her covers and convince herself to go to sleep.

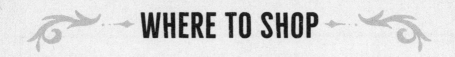

WHERE TO SHOP

Aunt Matilda's Steampunk Trunk, Gothic Shop
106 ST. GEORGE STREET

Do you ever just walk into a shop and know, instantly, that you are in the right place? This is how we felt when we entered Aunt Matilda's. Every shelf held something of gothic interest, from steampunk goggles to intricate gold clocks fit for a Victorian opium den. The employee who helped us was clearly a fan of the store (she also had a service dog that we were blessedly allowed to pet).

We recommend you check out the "About" page on Matilda's website before you visit, as the story of who Aunt Matilda is makes the store all the more charming. As the proprietor of the shop explains, Aunt Matilda was a force to be reckoned with. "In her lifetime, she visited the Torii gates in Kyoto, walked the Great Wall of China, hiked the deserts of Persia, and climbed the mountains of Tibet. She rode with a Romani caravan from Istanbul into Western Europe." In the spirit of Matilda, who collected trinkets during her travels, there is an array of treasures to choose from. Even if you've spent all your money by the time you get there, it's worth a visit. The purse collection alone is to DIE for, with motifs of coffins, bats, sugar skulls, Ouija boards, and more.

My Cauldron Too, Witch Shop

58 SPANISH STREET

There are several witchy shops in St. Augustine, so if you're on the witch side of goth you'll be pleased. We happened by My Cauldron Too as we walked downtown, drawn in by its name, *duh*, and its welcoming wraparound porch with seating. Less spooky and more green witch, the inside is sunny and smells great. There is an array of healing herbs and crystals, as well as tarot card decks, candles, and various altar supplies. As witches-in-training we were fascinated but maybe a little overwhelmed by the volume of items for sale. Thankfully there were handmade soaps to sniff as we considered our spell options.

WHERE TO EAT

A1A Ale Works

1 KING STREET

We ate dinner one night at A1A Ale Works, where we enjoyed a flight of Florida craft beer on the balcony of the restaurant before diving into our delicious meals. The restaurant overlooks Matanza Bay and boasts daily fresh fish selections, a thorough menu all made from scratch, and a rotating craft beer selection. We were lucky enough not to need reservations to get in, but calling ahead is always recommended, especially if you're visiting during a busy season.

O.C. White's

118 AVENIDA MENENDEZ

Another lovely dining experience we had was at O.C. White's, which not only featured fabulous food but is home to a haunted history. Built in 1790, the building was once a hotel and then a house, and it was moved to its present location in 1961. The ghosts of the original occupants, Mrs. Worth and her two daughters, have been seen, as well as the husband of one of the daughters. He appears in the mirror in the men's bathroom and is seen wearing a bowler hat. Workers have reported hearing voices and footsteps and seeing objects move on their own. It's a fun, historic place to eat, and we loved basking in the history of the place before devouring our meal.

Prohibition Kitchen

119 ST. GEORGE STREET

For lunch, before we departed on our last day, we stopped at Prohibition Kitchen. With a variety of small plates and the option to build your own burger, the restaurant gave us plenty of options and a nice atmosphere. We appreciate how their website describes it: "We offer you an escape into the clandestine, mysterious, and yes, illegal world of flapper dresses, speakeasies, moonshine, and swing. Sashay in and, let your senses be seduced. Let Chef Bradford's seasonally inspired techniques using local ingredients put the exclamation point on your rendezvous back in time." We enjoyed some deviled eggs and tap beer before heading back to snowy Minnesota.

Even as we were driving out of town, with a rideshare driver who happened to be from Wisconsin originally, we were already planning our return to this beautiful and unique city.

A WOMAN YOU SHOULD KNOW

Maria Mestre De Los Dolores Andreu

(1801–1860S)

Three years after Florida became a United States territory, a wooden lookout tower that had been used by the Spanish to defend their territory was converted into a lighthouse. At this time, lighthouses were the only way to keep mariners safe from hitting the rocky shores of America. In fact, lighthouse keeping was such an important job that only the U.S president had the authority to hire keepers.

Juan Andreu, the first Hispanic American to be inducted into the Coast Guard, was also the first keeper of the St. Augustine Lighthouse. When he retired, he gave the important job over to his son, Joseph. While keepers are desperately needed to maintain safety, they were compensated quite poorly for their work, so Joseph's wife, Maria, had to make do with gardening and caring for their children in the lighthouse on a small salary.

In 1859, Joseph was whitewashing the lighthouse when tragedy struck. He fell from the scaffolding, sixty feet, to his death. The community was naturally upset by the brutality of his death. It soon became clear that his widow was the only person with the knowledge and experience to carry on the lighthouse tradition. Soon, fifty-eight-year-old Maria Andreu was appointed as the lighthouse keeper, the first woman in Florida to earn this distinction. She is also the first Hispanic American woman to operate a federal shore installation AND the first woman (at nearly sixty, no less!) to be a Coast Guard employee. It's unfortunate that her husband's death had to occur in such a tragic manner for her to be appointed, but we're glad Andreu paved the way for many. The tradition of Hispanic Americans joining the Coast Guard has continued, thanks to women like her. Next time you pass a lighthouse, we hope you remember this absolute queen.

TRAVEL TIPS

1. Fly into the Jacksonville, Florida, airport to be closest to St. Augustine, or fly into Orlando and plan to rent a car. We were fortunate enough to find rideshares that took us for the nearly two-hour drive from Orlando but realized we would plan differently in the future.

2. St. Augustine is about five miles from the ocean, so plan for a rideshare or rental car to experience the shore. The town itself is extremely walkable, though, with plenty of shopping, food, and sights to see.

3. Wear comfortable shoes, especially if you're staying in the historic district, because there will be plenty to explore by foot within walking distance. Eat outside as often as you can, and take in that glorious Florida sunshine on your goth skin like we did.

4. Check out the online store for Mortem Manor (ShopMortem.com) so you don't have to pay for an overstuffed suitcase like Meg did.

5. Buy your pass for the Castillo de San Marcos early so you can use it for your whole stay.

OTHER SPOOKY PLACES AROUND THE STATE

Orlando

Orlando is about a two-hour drive from St. Augustine, and there is a good chance you may use the city's airport, as it's an affordable way to get to Florida. If you have time to spend in the land of theme parks, we have some suggestions to make it a spooky good time. Forget that cheerful mouse and get over to Mortem Manor, a rare year-round haunted house that genuinely scared us. It's a classic-style crumbling-mansion experience enhanced with unique scares, like a squishy floor that had us laughing as we figured out how to walk across. Meg took her husband, son, niece, and nephew, and it was the most fun she had in Orlando. Her husband (one of those people who watch horror movies through their hands) was so frightened he used their ten-year-old niece as a shield from the actors! Don't worry; she wasn't harmed by his lack of bravery. They also offer a coffin burial simulator, which we didn't have time for, much to the relief of Meg's husband.

Right next door is a dangerous gift shop—dangerous because you're going to want to buy it all. Meg, in fact, had to spend extra money at the airport on the way home because after this shop her bag was over fifty pounds. OOPS. But she came home with a werewolf purse, bat belt, Bruce Campbell gift for Kelly, and much more. Totally worth it.

If you find yourself with time in Orlando, make your way to Cocktails and Screams, the only Halloween-themed bar in the city. Besides monster-inspired drinks and decor, the bar features live music and other events. Make sure to swing by the bathroom, too, which features some of our favorite goth girls painted on the stalls: Lydia Deetz from *Beetlejuice* (1988), Wednesday Addams from *The Addams Family* (1991), and Nancy Downs from *The Craft* (1996).

Go on a Lighthouse Tour

Florida has several haunted lighthouses throughout the state, including one in Jacksonville and one in Pensacola. Take a walking or trolley tour in the cities you visit to get the most out of your visit.

Tampa Bay

If you're visiting the Tampa Bay area, book a room at the Phantom History House Bed and Breakfast. The home features a Victorian-style library, tarot readers, mediums, and nightly ghost stories. There are four themed rooms to choose from: the Cemetery Room, the Portrait Room, the Ouija Room, and the Castle Room (complete with remote-controlled flickering candles).

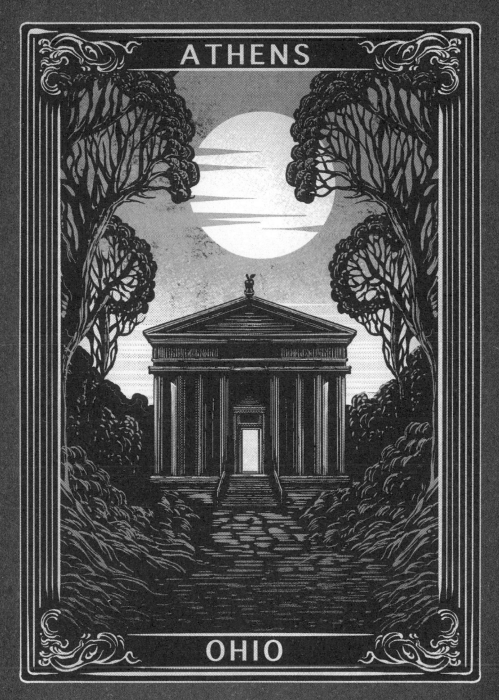

ATHENS

OHIO

POPULATION: 24,311

SPOOKIEST THING TO HAPPEN HERE

The Loveland Frog, also known as the Loveland Frogman, is described as a four-foot-tall humanoid figure that has been spotted in Ohio since the 1950s. Sightings of this creature have been reported by everyone from businesspeople to police officers, adding credence to the stories. According to Sam Jacobs, who was playing *Pokémon GO* in 2016, he saw something strange with his own eyes that was not part of the game. "We saw a huge frog near the water. Then the thing stood up and walked on its hind legs. I realize this sounds crazy, but I swear on my grandmother's grave this is the truth. Not sure if it was a frogman or just a giant frog," he said. "Either way, I've never seen anything like it." Although we didn't spot the Frogman while we were in Ohio, the stories made us intrigued to look out the windows of our rental car into the fields and marshes where he may have been lurking.

HIDDEN GEM WE DISCOVERED

Athens County Board of Elections

15 SOUTH COURT STREET

As we were walking one of the main thoroughfares of Athens, we passed a rather nondescript building. Normally we wouldn't give the Athens County Board of Elections a second glance. It's not the sort of fun saloon or grand hotel a ghost likes to haunt, and there's definitely not going to be any *Evil Dead* (1981) merch in there. Little did we know, we were passing the home of the biggest celebrity in Athens, Ohio, Pumpkin the cat! We stopped at the front window because we could see clues of a pet. There was a comfy bed placed right where a kitty could watch the world go by, a carpeted climbing tower, treats, and even paintings and posters of an orange tabby. Unfortunately, Pumpkin was busy with government work while we were there, but he is usually lounging in his bed to the delight of passersby.

The mascot of the Athens County Board of Elections is growing in popularity. "The preteen-aged rescue is a local celebrity in Athens near the Ohio University campus. His fans are mostly students and nearby residents, but his fame has already reached most of the state of Ohio. Even the Secretary of State's office asks about him." We'd like to think this autumnal-named cat is like the city of Athens's witchy familiar, there to be cute and add a little bit of magic and whimsy to downtown. Make sure you follow all of Pumpkin's official government work on Instagram @pumpkin_the_cat_fanpage.

MOST FAMOUS TRUE CRIME

Though inmates are no longer hanged or electrocuted in the electric chair known as "Ol' Sparky," the death penalty by injection is still legal in Ohio. Surprisingly, only three men have been sentenced to death in Athens County. The first was forty-three-year-old James Litteral, who in 1930 was convicted of the robbery and murder of miner Harry Green.

Green had returned home to Ohio from serving in World War I and was known in town as being "shell shocked and despondent." He would take long walks in the Kimberley Hills, where he was murdered by Litteral and robbed of several hundred dollars.

An article in Athens's *Sunday Messenger* described the criminal's final moments: "Litteral entered the death chamber shortly after nine o'clock. His request to be permitted to shake hands with all the witnesses was granted by Warden P. E. Thomas. To each of the witnesses he said, 'God bless you.' He then seated himself in the death chair, and before the electric current was turned on, he said, 'Lord have mercy.' The first charge was applied at 9:03 a.m., then another charge a minute later, and at 9:10 a.m., Litteral was pronounced dead by an attending physician." The other two men put to death in Athens were both electrocuted in 1950.

SPOOKY MOVIES AND BOOKS SET HERE

BOOKS

Beloved (1988) by Toni Morrison

The Outsider (2018) by
   Stephen King

The Rust Maidens (2018)
   Gwendolyn Kiste

MOVIES

A Nightmare on Elm Street
   (1984)

Heathers (1989)

The Faculty (1998)

 The annual Halloween block party held in Athens takes place on Court Street and has seen crowds as large as thirty thousand people in the past. Although we didn't personally attend, we spoke to people who did and confirm that it is a night to remember (or one you'll hardly remember depending on your consumption of alcohol).

WHAT TO DO

Ohio University

1 OHIO UNIVERSITY DRIVE

We had the opportunity to speak to a screenwriting class at Ohio University about our own experience and journey writing books, screenplays, and stage plays. We were thrilled to hear many of the students had their own spooky tales and recommendations of places for us to visit while in Athens. Haunted dorms, tales of ghosts, and eerie vibes down certain corridors no doubt inspire and play a role in the screenplays that are written in class.

Ohio University, founded in 1804, is the oldest college in the state. According to HauntedAthensOhio.com, West Green has been rumored to be built on top of Indigenous burial grounds. Wilson Hall, which was explored on the show *Scariest Places on Earth* in an episode titled "Satan's Dormitory," is considered the most haunted place on campus. The article also covers a dorm room in the 1970s that was reportedly the site of a woman practicing witchcraft and a mysterious death, and it's the only university room in the world that is sealed and closed. Residents of Wilson Hall report hearing voices and footsteps as well as seeing objects move on their own and lights flickering. Neither of us had the dorm experience in college, but now it makes us wonder what we would have experienced had we ventured that route ourselves.

Carrie: The Musical

19 SOUTH COLLEGE STREET

With a rotating schedule of plays, the OU theater was premiering their spring production of *Carrie: The Musical*. Based on Stephen King's novel from 1974, the play originally opened in 1988. Although it wasn't initially a critical hit, the songs and script were reworked, and the musical had a revival off-Broadway in 2012. Kelly had the opportunity to stage manage a production of the musical in 2019, and the score, message, and staging have stuck with her ever since.

In this musical set in the modern era, the character of Carrie is not only bullied in person but on social media as smartphones record her experiencing her menstrual cycle for the first time. Some of our favorite songs include the group numbers "In" and "A Night We'll Never Forget," and we swooned over the heartbreaking solos "Dreamer in Disguise" and "Once You See." The production was full of life, color, and talent, and we were so happy to be able to experience this Stephen King classic again while visiting Ohio. Other examples of plays the OU theater has put on in the spooky vein include *She Kills Monsters* and *Bloodknot*. Check out the always rotating schedule to find a dark gem.

 Columbus, Ohio, is the place Kelly first met James Marsters, who portrayed Spike on the *Buffy the Vampire Slayer* (1997–2003) series on television. She attended the Wizard World Comic Con and was able to chat with Marsters, get his autograph and several photos, and meet fellow fans throughout the event.

Athena Cinema

20 SOUTH COURT STREET

On the main street of Athens, you'll find the Athena Cinema, originally a grocery store, which was turned into a movie theater in 1915. The very first movie shown, Mary Pickford's *Cinderella* (1914), cost ten cents to attend. After a history of changing ownership and suffering a fire, the Athena was purchased by Ohio University in 2001 and is "operated by the College of Fine Arts at Ohio University as a three-screen, art house theater featuring independent, documentary, world, and classic films, as well as student and locally produced work."

It has also hosted the Athens International Film + Video Festival since 1974. The festival represents the values that Athens shares as a community by providing a platform for underrepresented voices and features a number of films including experimental, documentary, short-form, and animated. The festival is held in April annually, and while you're there, take a look around. Some locals reported eerie feelings in the theater, not related to the films they were viewing.

Visit The Ridges

100 RIDGES CIRCLE

"You have to go to the Ridges," said everyone in Athens, Ohio. Many of them admitted to sneaking into the abandoned sections of the building searching for ghosts. So, what are two morbidly curious friends to do? Actually, make that three, as our friend and OU theater alum Lisa Bol joined us. In theory, the Ridges is the haunted "lunatic" asylum of our wildest nightmares, the sort of place where anyone with a pulse could feel the stifling air of depravity. Yet, as we've come to learn through this journey, nothing is as simple as it appears.

Formally known as the Athens Lunatic Asylum and the Athens State Hospital, the building, which opened its doors in 1874, is now owned by Ohio University. Its current moniker is an obvious nod to the surrounding ridged hills from where it towers over Athens. It was a fairly warm afternoon for March when we came upon the enormous structure. As though it's the ominous setting of a Hitchcock film, the Ridges is a behemoth, every brick seeming to absorb the sunlight, casting shadows on its expansive lawn of about seven hundred acres. The hairs on our necks were standing at attention...until we were met on the porch stairs by Shawna Wolfe, vice president of university planning. From minute one it was obvious that Shawna had a deep passion for the restoration of the Ridges. As she gave us a personal tour of the connected buildings, we were inspired by her commitment to the Ridges's future, as well her hope that we were fair to its past.

When we entered the lobby, we were immediately met with a group of visiting OU students on an art tour. We slunk past, trying to blend in like ghosts ourselves so as not to interrupt their learning. The Ridges is now home to the Kennedy Museum of Art, which has rotating exhibits, including one about local flora and fauna that Shawna herself helped facilitate. Others focus on artists from marginalized communities, varying in still images, watercolor, sculpture, and other mediums.

If you want to visit the Ridges, the museum is a great way to witness an asylum that's been transformed into a place dedicated to beauty. There are also historical tours put on by the Southeast Ohio History Center as well as self-guided tours used in conjunction with the mAppAthens app on your smartphone. Telescope Nights is another way to get inside the former asylum. Free to the public, these events are held at the observatory late at night (around 9 or 10 p.m.), which seems like a great time to hang around the Ridges. If you don't bump into a ghost of a former patient, we can at least guarantee you'll see something pretty cool through the big telescope.

Because we were doing research on the Ridges, Shawna was nice enough to provide us a behind-the-scenes tour, for which we will be eternally grateful.

"I know what you want to see," she said. After meeting, it was obvious to Shawna that we were there for the creepy stuff. Sure, we enjoyed her positive spin, but we can't help but be intrigued by the secrets kept there, such as "the stain."

The stain?!

That's when Shawna told us the most notorious story associated with the Ridges.

In early December of 1978, Margaret Schilling, a patient at what was then known as the Athens Mental Health and Development Center, didn't show up for dinner. This led to the staff searching the grounds, to no avail. It wasn't until mid-January that the remains of Schilling were found in an empty room on an upper floor. She'd been locked in for a month and a half, in a part of the building that was not heated against the bitterly cold Ohio winter. While this tragedy could have been added to the tally of those who've lost their lives at the Ridges, Margaret Schilling left a literal mark.

Where she'd perished on the floor remains a stain to this day. What's more, this mark is in the shape of her body, an eerie visual memory of her death. Shawna told us she could not show us this mark, as the university is actively working to figure out how to restore that room while still showing respect to the deceased. If you're interested, you can find a photo of the unnerving spot online, as well as the science behind how it occurred.

Shawna gave us a thorough tour of the renovated areas, as well as works in progress. The grounds include hiking trails, and there's even cute, free-to-use mini golf on the outskirts. The most memorable part though, is the unrenovated side, where people are prohibited from going (as we learned from our chats with local friends, breaking into the Ridges seems to be an Athens rite of passage). Of course, we don't recommend this for many reasons, the foremost being that Shawna warned us before we went in that we'd be breathing in lead and asbestos. But she did suggest a short trip inside. Ah, the harm we put ourselves through to traverse the gothic landscape of Ohio.... Anyway, despite a frenzied call later to Meg's husband, who's a doctor, we did not die from poisonous air. His only question was whether we'd licked anything. We could say with confidence we hadn't.

Shawna led us over crushed drywall and littered bottles up a cracked staircase (right out of a horror movie) that could probably have given out at any moment and sent us straight to hell. We took a shaky video with our iPhone as we climbed up to the second floor. All of our filmic fantasies of skittering ghosts rushed through our minds. If you've ever played a game from the *Silent Hill* franchise, you could imagine what the abandoned floor of the asylum looked like. Every dark part of us wondered what the walls had seen. Our friend Lisa spoke of the oppressive energy, yet we felt only wide-eyed glee at the history. Shawna, on the other hand, looked upon the stained walls (just regular old-age stains, not dead-body stains), broken windows, and graffiti to see what the space could become. Apartments. Offices. Shops. We walked the length of the hall, surprised by the height of the ceilings and the amount of space given for the patients' common areas. Knowledgeable about the Ridges in every way—in fact, she'd helped clean it up in her undergrad years—Shawna told us about the Kirkbride approach to psychology, in which the architecture and area itself are used to heal the patient.

Despite the fact that Shawna has spent thousands of hours inside the walls of the Ridges, she hasn't noticed any spirits or felt negative energy. This made it all the more enjoyable when we were passing through a hall into a stairwell and the door opened on us unexpectedly. Shawna jumped and gave a little scream as the not-a-ghost-just-a-dude walked through. We all laughed together, defusing the tension. Who could blame her? She *does* work in an abandoned asylum.

Athens's Cemeteries

VARIOUS LOCATIONS

Before we left the property of the Ridges, we made a quick stop at one of its three cemeteries. Tucked into a wooded alcove, it offered a breathtaking, stark juxtaposition as the beautiful, sunny day shone on the simple graves of those who died at the Ridges. There is a quaint walking trail that weaves around the Old Athens Hospital Cemetery that will take you into the woods and out into a modern play park, complete with mini golf. This walk from the past to present will surely inspire your macabre curiosity.

The graves at this older cemetery are all marked with numbers instead of names, a rather disrespectful practice used until the 1940s, when those in charge at the Ridges decided to give their dead patients proper markers with dates and names. The Athens chapter of the National Alliance on Mental Illness (NAMI) has taken charge in a restoration process of the Ridges's cemeteries. As those dealing with mental illness, they are uniquely qualified to empathize with those who were institutionalized. Cemetery restoration is an involved process that includes history and genealogy research, as well as the proper maintenance of grave sites. We think this is a *perfect* way for us goth girls to restore history and therefore enrich our communities. Just as centuries-old buildings deserve to be taken care of, gravestones of those with no living family should be honored. We encourage you to seek out a local group that volunteers their time for grave restoration, so you can learn the best way to help in maintaining the history of the deceased.

If the Ridges doesn't give you your fill of cemeteries, then may we suggest Athens Cemetery on West Union Street. Quite a few locals told us about a rather famous grave marked with the statue of two young girls holding hands. Again, we were struck by the dichotomy of life and death as we stood at what should be a statue honoring the happiness of youth but is instead a monument to two sisters who barely got a chance to live. Donning matching dresses and pigtails in stone, the monument honors Erin and Jamie Downard, who died in 1989. It's believed that both girls were wheelchair bound with a rare genetic disorder that took their lives, so the statue is to celebrate their standing for the first time in heaven. Often, as we pass hundreds of gravestones with long-ago dates, or strangers' names, or simply just numbers, it's easy to forget how each headstone marks a human who had dreams. Someone who was loved and lived fully. This statue of the Downard sisters is a bleak reminder of the finality of death and its effect on us all.

Rumor has a way of making the rounds in a small town, and Athens, Ohio, is no exception. Several OU teachers, students, and citizens informed us that there was something darkly weird about the cemeteries in Athens: "They make the shape of a pentagram." This came up time and time again. Local legend was that whoever plotted out the cemeteries had a love for Satan and thus buried the dead in his favorite shape. Now that we have the powers of Google Maps (a lot cheaper than hiring a helicopter to take us up for an aerial view), we have to be the sticks-in-the-mud and say...um...we don't see it. Looks more like a curvy line to us. Oh well—cemeteries are creepy enough, right?

 The Monster Dolls Gothic Belly Dancers in Ohio "are a professional horror-themed, all-female group of entertainers that put on a choreographed show filled with lots of props, crowd interaction, and tons of fun! Each Doll has her own persona and is masked. We use many props, such as knives, swords, fire poi, staff, hoop, chairs, veil, along with a wide variety of monstrous props including TONS of blood! We put on an unusual circus-like show with many twists and turns!" Catch one of their shows or book them for your own event.

Hike to the Devil's Bathtub

CFP5+5X, LOGAN

If you're looking for an adventurous day trip, take the forty-five-minute drive to Hocking Hills State Park, where there are a number of creepy-sounding places to get lost in and be stalked by a forest witch, like Old Man's Cave, Tar Hollow, Whispering Cave, Grandma's Gatewood Trail, or, the most malevolent, the Devil's Bathtub. "Found between the Upper Falls and the A-Frame Bridge, the Devil's Bathtub is a bowl-shaped basin forming a whirlpool. The upper part of the falls drops into the tub of weak Black Hand sandstone and then drops again to a large pool below; it's been said that it goes into the depths of Hades." Does that mean it's more like a hot tub?

WHERE TO STAY

Hyde House Bed and Breakfast

138 FORT STREET, NELSONVILLE

There are plenty of reasonably priced hotels to stay at in Athens, some within walking distance of Ohio University. If you'd prefer to stay away from the youthful shenanigans of OU students, check out the Hyde House, a Victorian with a wraparound porch in nearby Nelsonville.

Connected to Athens by a wooded bike trail, the Hyde House was built in 1882. The historic home was first lived in by several doctors' families, then used as student housing and rentals, and finally converted into a B&B in 2006. There are several charming rooms to choose from, with names like Tulip Tree and Rose Garden. Our favorite feature? An epic spiral staircase that's just begging for you to walk down in your ruffled, high-collar Victorian gown.

 The Ohio Serpent Mound, located in Adams County, Ohio, is believed to have been built by the Fort Ancient people around nine hundred years ago. This protected historical earthwork is nearly a quarter of a mile long and represents a giant snake possibly holding an egg in its jaws. You can view the mound Tuesday through Sunday during visitor hours.

The Barn at Shamrock Farm

MANSFIELD ROAD

Another unique place to stay near Athens is the Barn at Shamrock Farm. The farmhouse-style home sleeps four, and you can watch the work happening on the farm and love on the family dog, Sam, while you're visiting. On the property, you'll have access to hiking trails, a creek, a patio with a grill, and a firepit.

WHERE TO EAT

Casa Nueva

6 WEST STATE STREET

After we spoke at Ohio University, we headed for a delicious lunch at Casa Nueva, which serves Mexican-inspired food. The restaurant, established in 1985 by unemployed restaurant workers with over a combined one hundred years of experience, is arguably Athens's favorite restaurant. Throughout their history, they have maintained ownership opportunities for all their employees. As their website reads, "At Casa, we believe that our efforts are part of a larger movement in which workers can provide direction and vision to create a workplace where all individuals are treated with equality, respect, and compassion." The afternoon consisted of a laid-back, quiet environment with delicious food and drinks in a comfortable setting. Reservations are recommended for weekends.

Zoe

24½ EAST STATE STREET

If you're looking for a laid-back, elevated environment for dinner while in Athens, consider visiting Zoe. On our first night in town, we sat down to a relaxing, delicious dinner that had plenty of options for meat eaters and vegetarians alike. Their website explains their name and mission: "*Zoë* means '*life*' in Greek. We believe that food is life. We see our food as the gateway to celebrate everything and everyone we cherish. So, here's to the moments we won't forget, with the people we will grow old with."

Little Fish Brewing Company

8675 ARMITAGE ROAD

After we visited the Ridges, Little Fish Brewing Company was recommended to us. A short drive away, the brewery has an alluring outdoor seating area complete with fire pits and decorated with lights. We enjoyed happy hour with drinks, snacks, and samples of brews that prepared us for the night ahead and gave us an insight to new establishments in the Athens area. Little Fish opened in 2015 and has a mission to support locally sourced ingredients for their food and beer, use solar panels and wind power credits for their electricity, and to support local economies. The brewery even has its own Airbnb in a nineteenth-century farmhouse located adjacent to the property. It is the perfect place to stay if you're traveling with a family or a group.

Jackie O's

22 WEST UNION STREET

There's a reason Jackie O's is featured in artistic renderings of Athens. It is a staple of fun, food, and pickle shots for locals and tourists alike. On the weekend, we had to wait for dinner seating but were able to enjoy local brews and wine at the bar before ordering food at our table. After our evening activities, we ventured back to Jackie O's for pickle shots, which are most similar to tequila shots. If you're taking a tequila shot, you lick salt off your hand, shoot a shot of tequila, then bite a lemon wedge. With pickle shots, you lick hot sauce off your hand, down a shot of vodka, and then eat a pickle! Delicious. Fun. And preferable (in our opinion) to traditional tequila shots.

WHERE TO SHOP

Passion Works Studio, Art Studio

20 EAST STATE STREET

Established in 1998, Passion Works Studio will immediately catch your eye as you're driving by in downtown Athens. The space is a collaborative community studio that allows people with and without developmental differences to make art together. They use upcycled materials that would otherwise be discarded, and every piece is led by those with developmental differences. We were able to tour the space, watch art being made, and purchase pieces to remember our time in Athens. The types of art vary from large puppets to small metal flowers, handmade bookmarks, and beautiful paintings. The passionflower is considered the official flower of Athens, and as soon as you see one, you'll begin to notice how much Passion Works has played a role in the aesthetic of the town. Patty Mitchell, executive director of the studio, describes their space perfectly: "We love things into a better place and want to love our community into a place that we want to live. We want people to come visit and experience it too." Stop by Passion Works to be inspired and support their amazing mission.

Uptown Costume Shop, Costume Store

12 SOUTH COURT STREET

Every day is Halloween in this crammed-to-the-rafters shop on Court Street. Need a black wig on a Wednesday afternoon? Sequined pants to go with your cape on a Friday? This place will hook you up. If you're a vintage diva willing to dig for treasure, Uptown Costume Shop could be the only provider of clothing and accessories you'll ever need. We flipped through an array of clothing sectioned by decade, and as a self-professed collector of sunglasses, Meg was overwhelmed by the many zany choices. Stars! Squares! Omg, black hearts! With a thriving theater community, the Athens locals get to be the true winners. See *Carrie: The Musical* and then wear her prom dress—pre-bucket of pig blood or after is up to you.

A WOMAN YOU SHOULD KNOW

Shawna Wolfe

As we mentioned in our tour of the Ridges, Shawna Wolfe is at the heart of the restoration of the asylum. At the start of our tour, she gifted us with the book *Asylum on the Hill*: *History of a Healing Landscape* (2012), by Katherine Ziff. Holding the book in our hands, we realized the weight of our responsibility to a place with so much history. It's easy as travelers to get caught up in the excitement, the temporary newness of a place. Yet, for Shawna, the Ridges is where she spends her working hours—a place, she admitted, she dreams about how she can make even better for her community.

In the New York City chapter, we talked about Nellie Bly, who is best known for her exposé on asylum life. In writing research for a past project, Meg read Bly's book and came away with a burning hatred for asylums, both in America and across the pond, where people, oftentimes women, were thrown against their will and left to rot.

Another book recommendation in the same vein is *The Woman They Could Not Silence: One Woman, Her Incredible Fight for Freedom, and the Men Who Tried to Make Her Disappear* (2021) by Kate Moore, a biography of housewife Elizabeth Packard, who was committed to an asylum in the 1860s in Illinois by a husband threatened by her independent spirit. Thanks to these books, shows like *American Horror Story: Asylum* (2012–2013), and the film adaptation of Nellie Bly's experience, *Escaping the Madhouse: The Nellie Bly Story* (2019), starring none other than goth queen Christina Ricci, we in the modern age are coming to fully understand the plight of women thrown into institutions because they were deemed inappropriate by the narrowest of measures.

In her article "Declared Insane for Speaking Up: The Dark American History of Silencing Women through Psychiatry" for *Time*, author Kate Moore gives examples of why some women were confined in asylums: they "had been committed for reading novels, for 'hard study' and for 'insane' behavior during the 'change of life.' (A woman's menstrual cycle alone could see her committed, suffering from 'uterine derangement.' Period-related madness was so commonplace that doctors encouraged mothers to delay the onset of their daughters' menses by making them take cold baths and abstain from meat and novels.)" If reading novels makes women insane, then we are certifiable.

Armed with this knowledge (and a healthy heaping of rage at the patriarchy), we were thrown off by Shawna's adoration of the Ridges. Instead of recognizing it as only a place for suffering, she is inspired by those who sought the Ohio hills for the healing property of nature. Shawna could see that the founders, the doctors, and the nurses were good people. Sure, not all of them—there are always bad guys—but as products of their time, they had a tiny fraction of the scientific knowledge we do today. They were working to heal, to make the world brighter, just as Shawna is working to restore the buildings for her community. She is in the process of turning a portion into senior housing and has dreams of turning outbuildings into local hangouts, like a brewery or event center. In our travels it's been easy, as ones drawn to the dark side, to recognize the murder, the pain, the disparity. Yet here was a fresh viewpoint, not one that disregarded the truth of asylums but rather saw the potential in making the structure into a home for art, beauty, and education.

TRAVEL TIPS

1. Be respectful of abandoned, reportedly haunted properties. It's important to get permission to explore or take a sanctioned, guided tour for safety.

2. Visiting the campus of Ohio University will give you all the feel of being a college student, and the fall, in particular, is a season to travel to Athens. The colors, leaves, and backdrop of the town make autumn a must-visit time to experience this small town.

3. While fall is the perfect season to travel to Athens, local sporting events and other festivals on OSU's campus can cause an influx of visitors, especially on the weekends. If you don't mind the crowds, book your stay well ahead of time.

4. We recommend renting a car while in Ohio. The ease of getting from place to place within the state in a rental car will allow you to see the breathtaking landscape, rolling hills, and charm of the small towns along your route. Plus, you'll have the flexibility to stop along the way at your leisure to shop, hike, or get a bite to eat.

5. If flying into Columbus, you can find a bus that will take you to Athens for as little as $10. There were eleven daily buses to choose from as of 2023, so you'll have plenty of options for arrival and departure times.

ACKNOWLEDGMENTS

Thank you to Erin, Todd, and everyone else at Sourcebooks!

Thank you, Stacey and Karmen, for your help and guidance and for championing our work.

Thank you to Lisa, Dan, Hailey, Josh, Erin C., Caissie, Stephanie, and everyone else who gave us tips on places to travel and things to see.

We appreciate our families for holding down the fort while we were traveling and supporting us in all our endeavors.

To our Rewinders, we'll see you in the horror section!

NOTES

Salem, Massachusetts

"to be the voice to the innocent": "About the Museum," Salem Witch Museum, accessed January 12, 2023, https://salemwitchmuseum.com/visit/.

"The first recorded reference": "The Old Burial Point," Charter Street Cemetery, accessed January 12, 2023, https://www.charterstreetcemetery.com/cemetery.

"Witch-hunters often had": Evan Andrews, "Seven Bizarre Witch Trial Tests," History, updated July 18, 2023, https://www.history.com/news/7-bizarre-witch-trial-tests.

"Because I could not": Emily Dickinson, *The Complete Poems of Emily Dickinson* (Boston: Little Brown and Company, 1960), 712.

"inspired by their lifelong": "About Us," Nocturne Salem, accessed January 15, 2023, https://nocturnesalem.com/pages/about-us.

"Though she apparently": Erin Blakemore, "The Mysterious Enslaved Woman Who Sparked Salem's Witch Hunt," History, accessed February 19, 2023, https://www.history.com/news/salem-witch-trials-first-accused-woman-slave.

Los Angeles, California

"softening of the brain": Thomas Samuel Duke, *Celebrated Criminal Cases of America* (San Francisco: The James H. Barry Company, 1910), 138.

"You're not going to": "The 'Lady in Black' Is Dead; Put Roses at Valentino Grave," *New York Times*, March 1, 1984, https://www.nytimes.com/1984/03/01/obituaries/the-lady-in-black-is-dead-put-roses-at-valentino-grave.html.

We interviewed our friend: Erin Carere, interview with the authors, February 20, 2023.

At age twenty-four: Natasha Leake, "Untold Secrets of the Hollywood Sign," *Tatler,* September 30, 2022, https://www.tatler.com/article/hollywood-sign-100th-anniverary-history-secrets.

"I am afraid": "Young Actress Ends Life in Hollywood," *Lewiston Daily Sun,* September 20, 1932, https://news.google.com/newspapers?nid=1928&dat=19320920&id=9oApAAAAIBAJ&sjid=gmYFAAAAIBAJ&pg=3051,5949013.

"The Dark Art Emporium": "The Dark Art Emporium," VisitLong Beach, accessed February 1, 2023, https://www.visitlongbeach.com/directory/dark-art-emporium/.

"evoke the magical aura": "Drink," The Cauldron Bar, accessed February 1, 2023, https://www.thecauldronbar.com/viewfullmenu.

"In my mind": "Explore," Castello Di Amorosa, accessed January 5, 2023, https://castellodiamorosa.com/explore/.

"the world's most unusual": "History," Winchester Mystery House, accessed January 5, 2023, https://winchestermysteryhouse.com/sarahs-story/.

Marietta, Georgia

"It almost moved": "Unknown 'Swamp Creature' Seen in the Okefenokee National Wildlife Refuge," Journal News.com, April 18, 2022, https://journalnews.com.ph/unknown-swamp-creature-seen-in-the-okefenokee-national-wildlife-refuge/.

"Many of the structures": Zoe Yarborough, "The Most Controversial and Haunted Lake in America: GA's Lake Lanier," Style Blueprint, March 24, 2023, https://styleblueprint.com/everyday/the-most-controversial-haunted-lake-in-america-gas-lake-lanier/.

Portland, Oregon

We asked Sarah: Sarah Gilbert, email to the authors, March 21, 2023.

"Local lore has it": Maya Seaman, "Portland's Shanghai Tunnels," *Travel Portland,* updated July 24, 2023, https://www.travelportland.com/culture/portland-shanghai-tunnels/.

"the best place": Camille Soleil, "Portland Is the Best Place in the Country to Be a Witch," *Willamette Week,* February 12, 2020, https://www.wweek.com/culture/2020/02/12/portland-is-the-best-place-in-the-country-to-be-a-witch/.

"Built by the millionaire": "Where Legends Stay," Benson Hotel, accessed January 20, 2023, https://bensonhotel.com/portland-hotel/history-of-the-benson-hotel/.

"Residents at the Massachusetts": Erin Blakemore, "Poorhouses were Designed to Punish People for Their Poverty," History, March 29, 2023, https://www.history.com/news/in-the-19th-century-the-last-place-you-wanted-to-go-was-the-poorhouse#.

"I wanted to": Andre Meunier, "A new look for Old Town Brewing shines a positive light on Portland—and its icons," *Oregonian*, January 13, 2023, https://www.oregonlive.com/beer/2023/01/a-new-look-for-old-town-brewing-shines-a-positive-light-on-portland-and-its-icons.html.

"I'm just super excited": Kyle Melnick, "'The Goonies' changed his life. He spent $1.6 million to buy the house," *Washington Post*, January 17, 2023, https://www.washingtonpost.com/nation/2023/01/17/goonies-house-movie-sold/.

Providence, Rhode Island

"They 'looted as much as'": Kyle Stucker, "Secrets, Serial Killers, and Mob Heists: True Crime Stories of New England," Providence Journal, updated September 16, 2021, https://www.providencejournal.com /story/news/2021/09/15/new-england-murder-true-crime-worthington -bish-entwistle-smart-dulos/5768255001/.

Austin, Texas

"Just as we got in": "Moore's Crossing," *What Was Then: Tales of the Unexplained*, August 14, 2011, http://whatwasthen.blogspot.com/2011/08 /moores-crossing.html.

"These taxidermy mounts": Micaela Jemison, "The World's Scariest Rabbit Lurks within the Smithsonian's Collection," *Smithsonian*, June 17, 2020, https://www.si.edu/stories/worlds-scariest-rabbit.

"We don't just want to be another": "About," Alamo Drafthouse, accessed March 9, 2023, https://drafthouse.com/about.

"One of my most favorite stories": "The Haunted Driskill Hotel," Austin Ghosts, accessed March 13, 2023, https://austinghosts.com/10-the-haunted -the-driskill-hotel/.

"In almost all these cases": Ker Than, "Chupacabra Science: How Evolution Made a Mythical Monster," *National Geographic*, October 30, 2010, https://www.nationalgeographic.com/culture/article/101028-chupacabra -evolution-halloween-science-monsters-chupacabras-picture.

"The rest of the season": Chris Hughes, "Austin Public Library Launches a Terrifying New Horror Podcast," *Austin Monthly*, April 13, 2023, https://www.austinmonthly.com/austin-public-library -launches-a-terrifying-new-horror-podcast/.

New York City, New York

"one study put": Xochitl Gonzalez, "New York's Rats Have Already Won," *Atlantic*, March 2, 2023, https://www.theatlantic.com/ideas/archive/2023/03/new-york-city-rat-infestation-politics/673250/.

"It was important to me": Dana Givens, "Cozy Up With a Book at this Bronx-Based Black-Owned Bookstore," *Black Enterprise*, February 26, 2020, https://www.blackenterprise.com/cozy-up-to-a-book-at-this-bronx-based-black-owned-bookstore/.

"I think all horror movies": Gabrielle Bruney. "Nia DaCosta Is Killing It," *Esquire*, August 27, 2021, https://www.esquire.com/entertainment/movies/a34334245/nia-dacosta-candyman-interview-2021/.

Duluth, Minnesota

"Some psychiatrists consider": "Wendigo—Flesheater of the Forests," Legends of America, updated December 1, 2022, https://www.legendsofamerica.com/mn-wendigo/.

Lake Superior is also known: Jim Richardson, "Lake Superior Sea Monster: Three Fatal Encounters," Perfect Duluth Day, August 14, 2021, https://www.perfectduluthday.com/2021/08/14/lake-superior-sea-monster-three-fatal-encounters/.

Established in 2006: "Mission," Catalyst Stories, accessed August 21, 2023, https://www.catalystories.com/mission.

Las Vegas, Nevada

"allows you to explore": "Tickets," The Mob Museum, accessed January 19, 2023, https://admission.themobmuseum.org.

St. Augustine, Florida

"The Florida heat in the middle": "The Haunted Tolomato Cemetery," Ghost City Tours, accessed February 1, 2023, https://ghostcitytours.com/es /st-augustine/haunted-places/tolomato-cemetery/.

Athens, Ohio

According to Sam Jacobs: "Are the Legends True? Man Claims He Spotted Fabled Loveland Frogman," WLWT 5, updated August 4, 206, https://www .wlwt.com/article/are-the-legends-true-man-claims-he-spotted-fabled -loveland-frogman-1/3568310.

"The preteen-aged rescue": Abby Jenkins, "Athens' Favorite Feline," *Post Athens*, November 2, 2023, http://projects.thepostathens.com/SpecialProjects /pumpkin-cat-board-of-elections-election-2023-issue-feline/. **An article in Athens's:** "Athens, Ohio Executions," Genealogy Trails, accessed March 19, 2023, http://genealogytrails.com/ohio/athens/newspaper/news_executions .html.

a woman practicing witchcraft: "Wilson Hall Room 428," Haunted Athens Ohio, accessed March 5, 2023, https://hauntedathensohio.com/wilson-hall -room-428/.

"Found between the Upper Falls": "Haunted Hocking Hills," 1st Choice Lodging, accessed February 1, 2023, https://1stchoicelodging.com/haunted -hocking-come-explore-the-spooky-side-of-the-hills/.

"had been committed for reading novels": Kate Moore, "Declared Insane for Speaking Up: The Dark American History of Silencing Women through Psychiatry," *Time*, June 22, 2021, https://time.com/6074783/psychiatry -history-women-mental-health/.

"are a professional horror-themed": "The Monster Dolls," The Monster Dolls, accessed March 10, 2023, https://linktr.ee/monsterdolls.

INDEX

⚚ ABOUT THE AUTHORS ⚚

Photo credit: Katrina Hanneman

KELLY FLORENCE and **MEG HAFDAHL**, authors of *The Science of Monsters*, *The Science of Women in Horror*, *The Science of Stephen King*, *The Science of Serial Killers*, *The Science of Witchcraft*, and *The Science of Agatha Christi*e are co-hosts of the *Horror Rewind* podcast, best friends, and lifelong horror fans.

Kelly Florence teaches communication at Lake Superior College in Duluth, Minnesota, and is the creator of the *Be a Better Communicator* podcast. She received her BA in theater from the University of Minnesota Duluth and her MA in communicating arts from the University of Wisconsin-Superior. She has directed, produced, choreographed, and stage managed for dozens of productions in Minnesota, including *Carrie: The Musical* for Rubber Chicken Theatre and *Treasure Island* for Wise Fool Theater. She is passionate about female representation in all media and particularly the horror genre.

Horror and suspense author Meg Hafdahl is the creator of numerous stories and books. Her fiction has appeared in anthologies such as *Eve's Requiem: Tales of Women, Mystery, and Horror* and *Eclectically Criminal*. Her work has been produced for audio by *The Wicked Library* and *The Lift*, and she is the author of two popular short story collections, including *Twisted Reveries: Thirteen Tales of the Macabre*. Meg is also the author of the four novels, *This World Is Nothing but Evil, Daughters of Darkness, The Darkest Hunger,* and *Her Dark Inheritance,* which has been called "an intricate tale of betrayal, murder, and small town intrigue" by *Horror Addicts* and "every bit as page turning as any King novel" by *RW Magazine*.